Presented to my dearest

Laxmi

Lake Singh

March 7, 2010

The Joys of Death

Death is viewed with much skepticism and distastefulness. Its often associated with excruciating pains and suffering—a bad and frightening act that is mechanical and dehumanizing. Sanctioned from scientific and scriptural viewpoints, this book will change your perceptions totally. Learn how to:

Conquer the fear of death.
Remove the trauma, anxiety and superstition.
Make it painless and easy on yourself.
Bring the god out of you.
Feel content to die.
Come face-to-face with God.
Enjoy the ecstasy and pleasureableness.

Death is but a sweet dream—a blessing in disguise!

Indo-Guyanese-Canadian, Dr. Lake Singh, having completed Pre-medicine holds: B.Sc. (Biology), B.Sc. (Chemistry), M.Sc. (Health Science), Doctorate (Longevity Health Science), Associate Degree (Business)—also studied Real Estate Law. www.thejoysofdeath.com

THE JOYS
OF DEATH

HOW TO CONQUER THE
FEAR OF DEATH

Dr. Lake Singh

**Munshiram Manoharlal
Publishers Pvt. Ltd.**

ISBN 81-215-1162-3 (HB)
ISBN 81-215-1163-1 (PB)
First published 2005
© 2005, **Singh**, Dr. Lake

Printed in India.
Published by Munshiram Manoharlal Publishers Pvt. Ltd.,
Post Box 5715, 54 Rani Jhansi Road,
New Delhi 110 055.

Dedicated to
My Mom, Dad, brothers Bisram,
Latchman, Dwarka, sister Drupatie
and in-laws Mr. and Mrs. Sarabjit Singh

Contents

Foreword

THE Joys of Death will forever change your life!
Dr. Lake Singh embarks on a course of uncharted
waters that would safely navigate you to journey's end—
take you across the ocean of mundane existence. These
long buried secrets unearthed here shall bring crowning
glory to your life.

Sanctioned both from scientific and scriptural viewpoints, he admirably supported his dissertation
throughout. And being the two most reliable ways of
decoding the universe, it's the best synthesis between
science and religion I have seen where grappling with
death is concerned.

The book is divided into several parts, building up to a
wondrous climax. It culminates with the exhilarating state
of *nirvana*—a word that is sadly misunderstood in the
West. It is the subliminal state of oneness with the Absolute—
the state of being where one makes peace with God.

To conquer death one must first master the Art of Living,
which is also given due consideration here. A life well lived
is a precursor to the attainment of liberation—for us to
benefit from the ecstasy that comes with fulfillment of our
human lives.

The decision to be (or not to be) a God is yours. And here
is your chance to make good of that resolution to become
divine—for you to obtain the highest recompense in life.

The book is worth its weight in gold. And I am delighted to be a part of it—to write the foreword to this colossus attempt. I have lived a full life of a-hundred years imbibing these very same principles expounded herein, which is sufficient testimony to their efficacy.

The Joys of Death speaks voluminously for itself. The book assuredly gives the wisest answers to life's most insidious question—death.

This is the closest you will come to know of the truth surrounding the mystery of life and death. Make no mistake about it.

My richest blessings to all.

His Holiness,
Swami Akshayanandaji Maharaj
President, Bharat Sevashram Sangha

Acknowledgements

I have a lot to be thankful about in my life. And I shall begin by thanking first and foremost God. Then come my sweet parents who brought me into this world: My beloved father Sriman Bechu Sangram Singh, and mother Srimati Padmani Devi. May God bless their noble souls!

I would next like to thank my guru His Holiness Swami Purnanandaji Maharaj of the Bharat Sevashram Sangha— a saint and sage of distinction who opened my inner vision and put me on the right tract in life. And next comes my *Sada Guru* (my guru's guru), a godman, Acharya Srimat Swami Pranavanandaji Maharaj whose life itself epitomizes the truth of the Holy Scriptures.

In his quest to achieve the highest status in life *nirvana*, he practiced austerity of a magnitude practically unheard of in modern times. In a book written by the internationally known author Professor Ninian Smart entitled *Prophet of a New Hindu Age*, he commented as follows:

> This book is an account of the life of the remarkable Bengali spiritual and practical leader Srimat Swami Pranavanandaji Maharaj who lived in the first half of the twentieth century—left his imprints on India in various ways. His type of penance is very different from that of other gurus and saints whose lives have come to the attention of the English speaking public. He stands most authentically for ancient Hindu values that can be easily overlooked by modern commentators, scholars and interpreters of religion.

Perhaps he is the most conspicuous case of austerity in modern times. It can be seen how rigid his self-discipline and training were. And quite apart from this, his accomplishments were of such that his life deserves to be better known than it is to the wider world. The achievements of the Acharya (or God working through him) were startling indeed.

We will take up this discussion again when we come to that single most important chapter dealing with *nirvana*. We would see how the Acharya realized the goal, which is to evolve a god out of man—to which he became a living testimony thereof.

The idea of writing this book dawned on me as a result of my close association with one of the Acharya's disciple His Holiness Swami Vijoyanandaji Maharaj. After listening to his ebullient and effervescent lectures on this very subject matter my mind was set to explore the possibility myself.

A special thank you to: Uncle Samuel Jhingree, brothers Hariram, Indarjeet, Chitradeo, Chetram, sisters Chitrawatti, Parbatty, Koosho, Kamal and best friend Naitram.

My source of strength is my beloved wife Savitri, my children Padma, Vishaul, Devita, Kenny, Arun, Kavita and my grandchildren Sangeeta, Rishi and Diya.

Special thanks to Dr. Sitansu Chakravorty and the wonderful Jain brothers late Devendra and Ashok of Munshiram Manoharlal Publishers.

DR. LAKE SINGH

Brampton, Ontario
Canada
30 March 2005

Introduction

"A walking shadow,
a poor player,
that struts and frets
his hour upon the stage
and then is heard no more.
It is a tale told by an idiot
full of sound and fury,
signifying nothing."

—Shakespeare

Is this all there is to it? A simple role in the drama of life! Like actors we strut and fret our hour upon the stage and then are seen and heard no more! And before you know its all over: The curtain falls and you gracefully make your exit without any fuss or fury.

And thus comes to an end too your temporary life, abruptly truncated even before you've had a chance to open your eyes to find out who you really are. For all you know it represents a short sojourn and brief span that flies through all too swiftly. Certainly not our home—we're all just passing through.

Does this insinuate then that we are such stuff as dreams are made on—our little lives rounded off with a deepsleep signifying nothing? You mean we are no more a walking shadow—our lives have no depth, meaning or significance. Is man just his skeletal or mortal remains?

But how can this be considering we are part of such a vast and intricate network of intelligence? Behold the marvel of the human machinery and the universe on the whole! Surely, there has to be more to life than what meets the eyes—more than what our senses can adequately perceive and comprehend.

INESCAPABLE QUESTIONS

Obsessed as we are with death, it poses many unavoidable and baffling questions: Who are we? Who were we before? Who were we even before we were we? Why are we here? But most important of all, where do we go from here. What promise does this Great Beyond holds for us?

In deep reflection and preoccupation thereto, we often cogitate and ponder over questions such as these only to turn inwards later on for answers that are not forthcoming. And finally we give up in despair and fall right back into a state of complacency, accepting life for what it is.

AN ENIGMA

The question pertaining to what happens to us after death had preoccupied the mind of man since time immemorial —that which has remained an enigma unto this day. And being of such a cryptic nature, it even haunted the gods of old we are told; speaking of which, was the pyramid too not a monumental attempt caste in stone?

Inevitable and inescapable as it is, death has undone countless numbers. Throughout the ages, people have all had one thing in common—their temporary lives came to an end. None has successfully fled from it—has yet lived forever.

No one really wants to die. But yet-for-all it's the most common phenomenon in life. And to compound matter even more, it's the least understood—reason being there's no substantial evidences available as to what happens to us after death.

THE QUAGMIRE OF DEATH

Formidable is fate! Without notice the tide could easily swing against us at any given moment. And much to our furore, dismay and lamentation, every second someone is dying. Families crowd around open graves to pay their last respect and tribute—watch in horror as their loved ones are being lowered into the cold earth.

This committal to our graves paints the darkest and bleakest picture of all. Trauma, gloom, despair over-shadow the bereaved ones left behind, wondering what it must be like to taste of death—what would become of the soul: Would it ascend to heaven, descend to hell, or remain just plain dead forever.

The malady of diseases, the decrepitude of old age and the bone chilling fear of dying and not knowing what lies beyond death's door, these all strike chords of mystery and uncertainty into the hearts of us all—make us want to cringe. Taking a heavy toll on us, it leaves us in a state of conundrum—bemused, bewildered and mystified all at the same time.

On account of this morbid phobia for the unknown (this hypochondriacal and pathological fear of death) man, in defiance thereto, just does not want to think of himself as being eternally doomed. No one wants to disappear into the fathomless abyss of nothingness—loses his personal identity that follows extinction.

And so that he may spare himself from any further psychological trauma thereof, man suppresses and stifles his feelings where death is concerned.

THE DYNAMICS OF LIVING AND DYING

The more one contemplates and thinks about death, the more wonderstruck he becomes: Why did the All-merciful and Compassionate Lord include it as part of the General

Scheme of things? But could you imagine what would happen if everyone was to live forever?

There would have been rampant, insurmountable problems: Overpopulation, chaos, confusion and corruption in general. And it goes without saying too that life would have been reduced to a state of drudgery making it not worthwhile living after all—monotonous, dull, boring and wearisome.

Death is included as part of the Great Design because it keeps everyone in check. Trying to win favors and please the Maker, man is thereby forced to accumulate good merits and virtues in his life. And this in the long run would make for a much better world.

But irrespective of what, there seems to be a higher purpose to life. Life is not just a question of survival—a mere privilege to live just for the sake of living. And as we would explore in greater details here, God has subjected man to what I would like to term a "cyclical merry-go-round"—one in which birth and death are included as integral parts and parcels thereof.

Dubbed the *Cycle of Birth and Death,* you are afforded a new opportunity each time to start afresh—to forge ahead until good fortune smiles upon you in your pursuit and attainment of the Supreme Goal.

And given time, even the galaxy will die a natural death, as is evident in *heat death*—a process whereby the stars energy literally gets depleted. But it revives itself all over again. Therefore, if the seemingly soulless cosmos has in place a built in mechanism to replenish itself, then why should man be any different—he who is full of life to begin with.

Death is that escape route Mother Nature so devises. Like the stars, the body too cannot keep on going forever. It will one day eventually breakdown, crumble and disintegrate. But like a rising star, man shall regenerate himself in a life more potent and sublimed.

Death for all intense and purposes could also be viewed as the perfect teacher—one whose lessons are the greatest you could ever dreamt of learning. And later on, we shall have the opportunity to hear from nonesuch but the Messenger of Death himself—the absolute pedagogue who never even minces his words.

WHO REALLY HAS THE ANSWERS

We know a lot about life for here we are living and experiencing it for ourselves. But about death we know little or nothing. To begin with, we've never had a taste of it! But why just presume there is no escaping the widespread, opened jaws of death—no way for us to defeat this illusive enemy.

Many of us are under the false notion that after we cease to be, there's no place for us within the four corners of the earth. Nay, not even in the Garden of Remembrance! We flatly deny any possible existence beyond the grave—the pulcher, the ossuary, the tomb, the internment.

And if not physically, isn't there any chance spiritually? Wouldn't it be great if after we die we could be reborn over-and-over again—until perhaps we attain the status of that of the gods or some other celestial beings! And who are we to say that this is not to be—that perchance we may even be re-united with our departed loved ones.

Even the great thinker Socrates concurred:

"To fear death, gentlemen,
is but to think oneself wise when one is not—
for it is to think one knows what one does not.
No man knows whether death may not even turn out to
be the greatest of blessings for a human being;

and yet people fear it as if they knew for certain
that it is the greatest of evil."

One may say that only the *dead* knows for sure whether or not there's life after death. But so too do the quixotic rishis and seers of India. And having done so in the greatest of details known to humanity, they made it their paramount duty to probe into the mystery of life and death.

Acting on their own idiosyncrasies, these sagacious sages of yore were bold enough to ask the ultimate question. And given the enormity and gravity of the situation, their inquisition saw them undertaking a thorough, systematic search into the Supreme Reality.

And fortuitously or not, it was through their serendipity that they were able to solve this most enigmatical, abstruse and recondite puzzle of all, which, in spite of its overall perplexity saw them being triumphant. And in furtherance thereof, they echoed and re-echoed their findings in the most jubilant and exultant manner: "Yes! We the Hindus have conquered death."

A COMMON MISCONCEPTION

The Indian civilization and wisdom of its seers up until recently have never been packaged and exported abroad in a meaningful way. And this has defeated the whole purpose of the game—a battle won by the insuperable rishis in arena of death the world knows nothing of.

Unable to grab worldwide attention, the underlining cause for this mishap must first be addressed. And to begin with, there previously existed a vast misconception about Hinduism: The outside world, through no fault of its own, viewed religion in India as a confusing tangle of myth—the worshiping of many gods and goddesses in countless forms.

But sadly enough though, this represents only the surface expression of the Indian faith. Beneath this superficial layer lies a pragmatic and highly evolved religion—one that cannot be simply dismissed, underscored, or taken for granted.

And as such, I shall take you with me in an exploratory journey deep down the unfathomable Indian Ocean of knowledge. And buried beneath there for centuries now is a priceless treasury—the unlocking of which shall reveal unto us the apocalyptic secrets of life and death.

However, before commencement of this journey, a few introductory remarks would be quite in order here. And as much would be relied upon in terms of references to the sacred texts of the Hindus, I shall give you a bird's eye-view of the more important ones, namely the *Gita* and Upanishads.

THE GITA

The *Gita* is the spoken words of God—words that emanated directly from the lips of the Blessed Lord Sri Krishna. It is a text with an essentially timeless message meant for all humanity. Inasmuch as the Blessed Lord Jesus and the *Bible* are to Christians, so the Omniscient Lord Sri Krishna and the *Gita* are to Hindus.

The *Gita* is one of the greatest religious documents ever tendered. Declared the crystallization of knowledge, it is considered the essence of the four Vedas (the oldest scriptures of the Hindus) and all other texts put together. It's a gospel that has profoundly influenced the lives of the Indian people including that of the great Mahatma Gandhi.

In it the Lord related the *yogas* which are the prescribed pathways leading to union with God. And some 5,000 years ago these primeval teachings were presented to humanity in form of a dynamic dialogue between Sri Krishna and his prized disciple Arjuna.

UPANISHADS

The Upanishads represent the perennial philosophy of the world dating as far back as the second millennium before Christ. And incisive as they are today, how long they were handed down as part of an oral tradition can only be conjectured.

The authors were not just mere philosophers but the much gifted rishis of ancient times—chronicling whose life is a sheer delight. Having recorded in the annals of the Upanishads their invaluable personal experiences and divine encounters with God, the Upanishads became known as the *gemstones* of knowledge.

Being the memoirs and séance of these great intellectual minds, the Upanishads have contributed much to our understanding of the underlying reality of the world. Filled with such pure archaic wisdom of yore, they became popular and renowned in the Hindu world.

Not just some pundits, but extraordinarily powerful progenitors were the avid rishis. Being of such profundity and fastidious nature, they bluntly refused to succumb to any problem confronting them. And in demonstration of this pioneering spirit, they had risen to the challenges facing the human race on several occasions.

They were men of good deportment—possessed impeccable characters beyond reproach. And in addition to belonging themselves to the class intelligentsia, they also had going for them great proclivity for religious matters. They were men of such astute, spiritual acumen that they were considered next to God.

Of such rectitude and probity were they then that these "seekers of truth" became votaries of immense power. And where majority would fall head-over-heels over the acquisition of material power, these saintly men of God were more concerned with building their power of Self-awareness.

Whereas the homes of ordinary men were adorned with coffers for storing money and other materialistic valuables, theirs were filled with the wealth of knowledge—the treasure house of many imponderable spiritual secrets so garnered and stashed away.

Studying the hagiography of these nonpareil and honorific masters, they ought to be enlisted for the greatest citations of all times! In fact, their hagiology will become even more glaringly clear here, where interspersed throughout this book are anecdotes on their life and times.

Inimitable as they were, had it not been for them we would perhaps still be groping in darkness where the phenomenon of life and death is concerned. And having shed much light in this regards, humanity shall remain eternally grateful to these singularly most distinguished souls.

❋ *Part One* ❋

INVITATION TO A HIGHER REALITY

Objectives

In the following three chapters our statement of objectives would be as follows:

Playing the Game of Life Safe
Before embarking on this exploratory journey, I shall endeavor to establish here a clearer understanding on the true perspective of life. Then, we shall determine why it becomes imperative for us to believe in a Supreme Being.

The Art of Living
In this chapter it is my settled intention to lay a solid foundation on the true purpose of life—as well as to introduce the topic "How to know God." And if I may add, conquering death has a lot to do with mastering the Art of Living.

Mind Above Matter
Taking you on a journey through the regions of the mind, we shall arrive at a place that represents invitation to a *Higher Reality.*

✳ *One* ✳

Playing the Game of Life Safe

THE QUESTION OF PROOF

MAJORITY of us do believe in some form of life after death. But the question is that of proof: How do we do so beyond the shadow of a doubt? And as a result of our inability to come up with the necessary supporting evidences, we tend to place further inquiry into obscurity.

Realizing that these theories must withstand the rigors and scrutiny of scientific reasoning, we become further troubled knowing they don't—lack of which results in us getting no where in our quest for answers.

As rational human beings we would sooner accept empirical evidences rather than any other forms of validation. In other words, the only measure of validity is science. But first it must be determined whether or not it is within the scope of science to do so, which, quite unsurprisingly enough, evokes a negative answer.

But before we look at the logics behind this premise, there're two basic assumptions we have to make and rely upon. And upon further clarification and analysis, we shall then learn why scientists cannot prove nor disprove the *Theory of Life after Death*.

THE TWO BASIC ASSUMPTIONS

The first assumption we would make is that the Magnanimous Father pervades the entire universe—the one Omnipresent Lord found here, there and everywhere. And the other assumption has to do with the fact that whereas God's magnanimity is found expressed as the Universal Soul, man's is seen as the individual soul—the latter being a mirror image or reflection of the former.

But what we may not realize is that science is unable to prove nor disprove the existence of God. And by inference then, this would also hold true for the soul—it being essentially no more part God in man.

As you would imagine, there has to be a very good reason why God has kept it a secret from us. And if I may venture to guess, it would be to say that: The ways of the Lord are inscrutable. Perhaps it's His way to find out just how strong our faith is in the Absolute.

RELIGION VERSUS SCIENCE

Before we attempt to settle once and for all the question pertaining to the existence of God and the soul, let me reminisce by sharing with you some invaluable experiences I've had during my formative days—findings that would make you want to think of life as being brutal, truculent and brusque.

Quite young and immature at the time, I found that the question of death bothered me tremendously. I thought to myself why the imposition of such a harsh and cruel treatment. And coming too from a God we all look up to as being just and fair, what's the point in Him bringing us into this capricious and whimsical world simply to be taken away in the end, never to be seen and heard from again!

The more I thought of it, the harder I tried to lead a life that pleases God. I thought to myself that this would perhaps be the safest and best route to take, hoping to be rewarded one day when I need it most—the day when comes my turn and I am called upon to answer to Him.

But it occurred to me too what if religion does not hold true to its promise. What if all this talk about there being a God turns out to be no more a big hoax—a farcical *Belief System* designed out of fear for the unknown.

Or, having an underlining political motive, what if it was invented by the Founding Fathers in order to instill fears into our hearts. That by calling for the decent of the wrath of God for our sins and infractions, man would not want to suffer any of the dire consequences. But really speaking, there is no God.

Therefore, the thoughts of exploring science grabbed me as a much better alternative—bearing in mind that scientific theories are hard core proven facts and not just mere guesses or hearsay. So here I was faced with these two possible choices—science versus religion.

The question though was which of the two bears the truth. But little did I know at the time, the Vedas were as scientific as one could get. As a matter of fact, in certain areas it even surpassed and outdistanced science by leaps and bounds.

After due deliberations I was more inclined to go the science route in my investigation. To begin with, I felt it was far ahead of religion and perhaps the most prudent and rational thing to do. So I resolved to take to the highest possible form of learning by becoming a student of science and a medical doctor.

I just couldn't wait to explore the human biology in all its sophistication: The composition, the physiology, the mind, and the soul. And equally so too, I was eager to learn what transpires during the clinical aspects of death. That perchance there's exist a way to avert the process altogether—a chance to stave off my own death!

LIMITATIONS OF SCIENCE

Hence I began my studies at Minnesota State University. I was enrolled in Pre-medicine which I successfully completed, but not before my startling discovery.

In one of my Biology classes I found out exactly why scientists were unable to prove nor disprove the existence of God, and, for that matter too, the soul as well as we would see later on.

As a footnote, please permit me to walk you through the process here. To conduct a Science Experiment you are required to set up two identical stations in every which way possible, save and except for the variable(s) that is the subject of the experiment. And in illustration thereof, let's look at this rather over simplified version of a typical Science Experiment.

If, for instance, we need to demonstrate the effects sunlight has on plants, all we need to do is simply take two plants: One exposed to the sun and the other kept in the dark. By showing that the one receiving sunlight flourishes while the other withers, you would have thereby scientifically proven that sunlight indeed makes a difference.

In setting out to conduct a similar experiment where the existence of God is concerned, you would similarly be required to set up two identical stations in every respect, save and except you need one scenario where God is present and another where He isn't. But here comes the big dilemma!

If there is indeed a God, then He would be everywhere at the same time, seeing that He is the Ubiquitous and All-pervading Lord of the universe. And that being the case then, how would you create a controlled environment where He is not present?

If by the same token there isn't a God, then how would you manage an environment where He is present? Impossible as it is, this has led to man's utter failure to invade the privacy of Him who is within the precincts of His Cosmic Hiding Place. It leaves the mysterious and abstruse Personality of Godhead unprovable!

In admitting defeat, here's how your average scientist would intelligently address the issue: *God is beyond proof. He's outside the reach of measurement and quantification, let alone be comprehended by our limited, earthling minds.*

Getting back to our discussions, it was a shocking discovery for me; having made which, it immediately dawned upon me to take a closer and more objective look at religion. And not only because its the older of the two branches of learning, but it seems only natural too to believe in a Supreme Being.

Religion and Science are not mere opposites but just different ways of decoding the universe. Having come to this realization, I began looking for clues to see whether or not Religion has any form of scientific validity at all. And the more I probed into the matter, the more obvious it became that the Hindu Religion in particular stands up rather well to the scrutiny of science—that in many facets of human learning it has even preceded and eclipsed Science.

SURYA NAMASKAR (SUN WORSHIPING)

As a random sampling, take *surya namaskar* for example! Hindus have been worshiping the Sun-god Surya for eons now—a practice still very much in vogue today. They firmly believed in their hearts that the sun is of paramount importance to man's survival—convinced of which they daily worshiped it as a living entity or god.

Today it has been proven beyond the shadow of a doubt that the sun is indeed the source of all life here on earth.

Without sunlight, plant growth would not be possible. And without plants, where would the animal kingdom be—completely obliterated and extinct I opine!

The unerring rishis were brilliant enough to have realized this subtle truth. And in stipulation thereto, they instituted a method to worship and enhance the benefits of the sun, which, because of the lack of space, we cannot get into any further details here.

EXERCISE IN FUTILITY

I realize too how futile it would be if we were to simply sit back and wait upon science to prove everything. There would be the risk of us running out of time—tread on risky and dangerous grounds. And here's a concrete example of what I am trying so hard to convey to you.

Having established the fact that there's no scientific or quasi-scientific way to prove the subsistence of God, the same can be said too about the soul. For as much as the soul is the representation of God in man, the only conceivable difference between the two lies in degree: While God is vast, the soul is minuscule.

So just as we are unable to prove the inevitability of God, the soul remains illusive just the same—suggestive of the fact that scientists may never be able to trace the impending destination or posthumous fate of the soul. It simply doesn't lend itself to this type or mode of investigative scrutiny.

DON'T WAIT UPON SCIENCE

The bone of the contention is that we do not have all the time in the world. Even that which we have flies through all too swiftly. And taking into consideration too that man spends practically a-third of his life in the unconscious sleeping state, there remains not much we can account for in life.

If we're to wait upon science, we would be eluded by time and overtaken by death—live under the false hope that science would one day give us the satisfaction of proof when in fact this may never come to pass.

Come to think of it, no body would undertake a religious life if there is no one looking over his shoulders—someone constantly keeping an eye and passing judgment on him. Wouldn't this be a royal waste of time?

But what if there's a God, which in all probability there is? Why gamble and have our lives exposed like this—allow ourselves to become deceived, cozened and outwitted by fate? And what a price to pay too if it turns out that we are in fact wrong in our assumption about God!

After much deliberations and circumnavigation, I finally came up with a theory of my own called *Playing the Game of Life Safe*. And the more I thought of it, the more I found it foolhardy not to take the necessary precautionary measures—have in pace a *contingency plan* of my own.

After all, why would I want to squander this golden opportunity—leave my life totally up to chance. Instead of accepting a subhuman or defeatist type of attitude, why must I not cultivate positivism—deploy everything I have at my disposal in waging this war in the battle of life?

BE A GOOD SPORT

Why would I not want to turn to God—my sole refuge, protégé and support in life? Why must I not trust Him and the universe; commune and maintain contact with Him; implicitly obey His divine laws and follow their directives—have blind faith in Him?

If we do not walk in the fellowship of God, our plot in life shall be filled with thorns—path lined with pebbles! Vulnerable as we already are, why not have our lives insulated against the many odds there are against us—accentuated, entrenched and brought under the aegis of the Supreme Spirit.

God suffers us not to go against His Behest and Holy Establishment. Rather, we should subject ourselves to one another and God. But in abeyance thereto, man has brought upon himself a state of adulteration; having to avoid which, he has deputed His One and only son.

And in the most befitting manner he enjoined unto man as follows—a clarion call or caveat man must not take too lightly:

> *"If ye continue in my word*
> *then ye my disciple indeed;*
> *and ye shall know the truth*
> *and the truth, shall set you free.*
> *Verily, verily. I say unto you,*
> *if a man keep my saying,*
> *he shall never see death.*
> *And this is the will of him that sent me,*
> *that anyone which seeth the son*
> *and believeth in him,*
> *may have everlasting life;*
> *and I will raise him up at the last day."*
>
> —*The Holy Bible*

God so love the world that He gaveth His only begotten son so that anyone who believe in Him shall not perish but have everlasting life. Following in the footsteps of God, one can live his life in abundance—fully imbued and richly embellished in Him whom we ought to trust and love.

After all, what does it profit a man to gain the whole world but loose his very own soul! How unfortunate it is for those of us claiming we use immortality as a means of comforting ourselves—wanting to escape the harsh reali-

Playing the Game of Life Safe

ties of death! I agree, we all shall have to die one day, but what if this is not true in a spiritual sense.

And getting back to our theme here, if in fact it turnouts there is no God, then no harm done. That would be the end of that. Seeing that there is no one to punish us for so falsely believing, man is free of all misgivings. No repercussion or harm can come to him anyway!

But remember, if you don't have a ticket, you don't have a chance. And in playing the *Game of Life* safe, you would have afforded yourself this wonderful opportunity—perhaps have in your hands the winning ticket. You have absolutely nothing to loose, but everything to gain.

ATHEISTS AND THE NON-BELIEVERS

Placed in an ominous situation such as in the throes of death, how strange it is that when all else fail even the impenitent agnostics would instinctively call out to God for help. Doesn't this tell us something only all too glaringly clear: Our souls yearning for the divine programmed right into our subconscious minds—a paganism having not a leg to stand on!

In spite of such nescience and impertinence, the All-merciful Lord still affords the apostates and heretical miscreants an opportunity to make amends to their impetuous and incorrigible ways. God advocates its never too late for any of his children to repent of their sins— tardily apologize and make confession thereof.

Oh man, no matter what mitigating or extenuating circumstances there might have been in your life, do not wait any longer. Act now and play the *Game of Life* safe. In you resides super human strength. Make full use of it. Treasured are you in the sight of God—a rare find and precious gem indeed.

In the next chapter, we begin with this postmortem: An

in-depth analysis of what the Lord might have had in mind when he first created mankind. And with this, I trust man would live his life as exemplified by His trusted emissaries—charter a safer course so that posterity may judge.

✤ *Two* ✤

The Art of Living

IN THE BEGINNING

I will give you the word all scripture praise.
That word is Om.
That word is the highest.
That word is God.

—The Upanishads

IN the beginning was the *word* and the *word* was with God, as is mentioned in the *Holy Bible.* And the inference here then is that this *word* could not have been just any ordinary word—a presupposition further substantiated here by this Testamentary declaration: "Without this word was anything made that was made."

And in concurrence thereto, Hindus too believe that the fundamental basis of creation can be ascribed to the word *Om*—the one and only sound found at the dawn of creation. And being that *Om* existed before everything else, it makes it truly primordial—that which was there right from the very commencement.

Being the sum total of all cosmic sounds, *Om* is seemingly interminable and highly potent. In it was found compressed divine intelligence. And when came time for the birth of the universe, this mother-sound broke the cosmic silence and give rise to many sub-frequencies; implying that this word somehow got transformed into an enormous amount of matter and energy in the form of creation.

THE MANIFEST AND UNMANIFEST

"In the beginning was neither existence nor non-existence.
All of this world was in the form of unmanifested energy!"
—*Rigveda*

Looking at it from a different angle, we are taught that before creating this world God was alone—God in form of his unmanifested energy. And since He was alone, it is only logical to conclude that everything came directly from him—seeing that it was He and He alone at the beginning and nothing else.

And taking into further consideration that you cannot get something out of nothing, it certainly makes perfect sense. And this implies then that everything from onset did in fact possess an element of God—a premise we shall develop further in due course.

Hence, this confirms the Hindu belief to be correct—the fact that God is found inherent in everything be it animate or inanimate. It finds fulfillment and support both from a Biblical as well as a logical point of view. And, being immanent in everything means that this world is an exhaustive revelation of God, which in the final analysis, makes us all divine beings.

However, even though God is found inherent in everything, He is more revealed in the animate than in the inanimate—more in the conscious than the unconscious. And in the animate, He is more pronounced in man than any other forms of life. And among men, the divine spark burns brighter in the good rather than the evil minded.

God so loves man that He created him in his own image and likeness. Taken out of the dust of the earth, he breathed into man *the breath of life* and man became a *liv-*

ing spirit or *soul.* And malleable or pliable as he is, God has so molded and shaped him like he did to no other.

Having full confidence in man, the Good Lord even went further in crowning him *king of his creation*—gave him dominion over everything. And he further endowed him with all superior faculties of speech, intellect and discrimination—privileges forthrightly devoid in the lives of all others.

In the *Holy Bible* there is this affirmation:

> *"Let us make a man—*
> *someone like ourselves*
> *to be the master of all life upon earth*
> *and in the skies and in the seas.*
> *So God made man like his Maker.*
> *Like God did God make man."*

And God even bestowed upon man the finer qualities of love, patience, decency, and compassion—seraphic and deistic traits conferred solely upon man only. And these, if I may add, serve to set him further apart and ahead of all other created beings.

God saw man, was pleased, and declared him to be good. In the eyes of God man is the manifestation of divine beauty. And in all adulation and praiseworthiness, this led Him in appointing man his prized representative upon earth—realizing which man ought to lead a life that befits his divine calling.

Making it incumbent upon man to offer protection to all, God entrusted him and no one else this fiduciary duty. This God-given privilege confers upon man the duty not to hurt, but to love—to be a good shepherd that keeps a watchful eye over His flock.

Oh man, you cannot do just as you please or see fit. You are the salt of the earth—a worthy instrumentation in the hands of God. Let your light shine before men that they may see your good deeds—the crest jewel of God's creation that you are.

MAN'S EARLY BETRAYAL OF HIMSELF

Instituted for man is a divine Plan of God. Right from the very beginning, God wanted man to emulate Him in every which way humanly possible. But although He had this kind of faith and belief in man, He nonetheless thought it fit to put him to the test early starting with Adam and Eve.

But on account of their nefarious scheme and act of impropriety, they both failed him. And in obliquity thereto, they fell prey to man's eternal foe in the form wanton disbelief—committed a much indictable offence. And showing no clemency, the Lord pronounced upon them a vehement curse.

They were ordered not to eat of the forbidden fruit in the Garden of Eden. It was made specifically cleared to them that if they do, it would be made peremptory for them to die—doomed to death if they so disobeyed the Lord! And though perhaps done in a nonfeasance and perfunctory manner, it nonetheless led to man's eternal damnation and perdition.

From the very inception of time, the recalcitrant human race has been taking to the wrong path—going further and further adrift from the Creator. Or, it is just that we have been simply hiding from God—become forgetful of our true divine nature, purpose and mission in life.

And not only have we forgotten the aims and objects of life, but more so got caught indulging in the frivolities and trivialities of it all. Aimlessly and heedlessly have we not been concentrating on sentry duties only—inattentive to this higher and nobler goal set for us by God?

FOR THE JOY OF LIFE

Quite indicative of the fact then, we seem to have lived our lives below our true potential—just a mere fraction of what our human capabilities are. And though possessed of many nascent talents and abilities, it is not surprising that we pass through all of life not knowing who and what we really are.

What is missing is the need for a higher form of living —a mode of simple living and high thinking just as was prescribed in primeval times by the impeccable rishis. And if lived within these parameters, life shall blossom in all its beauty and splendor—being that a life well lived is one firmly rooted in God.

THE GOAL OF LIFE

We are the embodiment of all that is good and virtuous. Hence, we must not accept anything less from what life has to offer us. Given its paraphernalia, the *Theory of Divine Immanence* states that Hinduism aims at gradually unraveling the divinity that is inherently man's.

God wants man to become perfect even as the Heavenly Father is perfect. After all, which father wouldn't want his son or daughter to be just like him, if not better! What is more ennobling and gratifying to a father than the welfare of his very own flesh and blood!

Hence, we arrive at the foremost principle or spiritual necessity: The need to forge and build an amicable relationship and sweet rapport with God—to impersonate and emulate Him in every way. Nothing would please the Lord more, as would also our earthborn biological father.

There could be no other purpose the Lord had in mind when He first created man other than for him to become a veritable god himself. And mark you, not just some demigod too! Man is destined for perfection—he who shall walk the face of this earth to the full credit and glory of his

Maker!

The goal of life then is not merely to humanize, but in fact deify and make man holy—to apotheosize, educe and evolve a *god out of him!* And if we were to translate any of this, it would spell heaven on earth.

Hence God exhorted and beckoned unto man:

*"Blessed are those who become what is Godlike.
Let a man raise himself to the status of the gods.
Let him not debase himself."*

—Sri Krishna

Each one of us is like a young eagle, soaring higher and higher until we reach the glorious sun. Life's primary purpose can be met with resounding success only if we were to reach out and become Godlike. Thus the rishis have coined the word *yoga,* meaning "to yoke" or become one with.

We must come to the ultimate realization that we are sparks of the divine. And the purpose of us being here is simply to enhance and make good that divinity, so that we may become pure enough to enter the unitive state with God—a process whereby our individual soul gets merged with the unadulterated Universal Soul.

It's like at birth you are given a precious piece of diamond, which upon the end of life's journey you are asked to return to the giver. And mistaken it to be artificial in nature, some of us may return it in the same manner it was given to us. Some in a worst state. While those of us who are fortunate enough to realize it's true value, may return it as a sparkling piece of jewelry!

And so too it ought to be with our lives! This *spark* (the soul) that rightfully belongs to God must, upon return, be in the purest and most reflective manner—like a brilliant piece of diamond. Then He shall be most pleased with us— bless us with His very own hands!

MAN—THE TEMPLE OF GOD

What else could this body of ours be but a holy shrine or temple of God, wherein dwells the Lord in the innermost recess of our hearts. Behold, the kingdom of God is within each and every one of us—man having not to look anywhere externally to find God!

Here St. Paul gives this very definitive answer in form of a strong ultimatum. And in so doing, he first filed an interdiction and formal prohibition notice before seeking the appropriate injunction order against man—a command for him to abstain from all acts that would defile this holy tabernacle:

> *"Know ye not that ye are the temple of God,*
> *and that the spirit of God dwelleth in you?*
> *If man defile the temple of God*
> *him shall God destroy*
> *for the temple of God is holy*
> *which ye are."*
>
> —*The Holy Bible*

SPIRITUAL DISCRIMINATION

What sets us apart from all other living creatures is our ability to think and discriminate. And making full use of these enormous faculties shall set us free from the bonds and shackles of death—wherefore God wholeheartedly promises that He shall see to it that no harm comes to him who adheres to spiritual truths.

God commendably looks upon those individuals as dearly as his very own self. The Lord Sri Krishna extols the virtues of such pious and reverential souls. And here's this compendious account:

> *"There are four kinds of men who worship me:*
> *The world-weary, the seeker of knowledge,*

the seeker of happiness and
the man of spiritual discrimination.
The latter is highest of them all.
He is continually united with me.
He always devotes himself to me and no other,
for I am very dear to that man
and he is dear to me.
Certainly, these are all noble
but the man of spiritual discrimination
I see as my very own self!

RIGHTEOUS LIVING

What really counts is not dogma but conduct. Religion is not so much *Correct Belief* as it is *Righteous Living*. And having given due consideration thereof, it makes it rather imperative for us to build a life that pleases God—our character being the monolithic fortress on which rests a well constructed life.

And since character is fortified by thoughts (as one thinks so he becomes) it behooves us to think and contemplate daily on God. And we must continue doing this until the highest revelation dawns on us—until we find the prevalence of God in our lives at every step on our way back to Godhead.

The Lord also bade man to show sympathy and compassion to one another. Buddha is quoted as saying. "To understand all is to forgive all." Without great loving kindness and a compassionate heart, the gates to our deeper consciousness would never be rendered open unto us—indicating that one should never leave kindness and compassion for tomorrow.

There can be no rancor nor hatred in our hearts or else we would not be able to come face-to-face with the Superlative Father of unsullied love. Rancor and hatred shall divide us against ourselves. And a house so divided cannot stand by itself, asserted the most Benignant Lord! Less you humble yourself like a child, you cannot enter the Kingdom of God.

Thus Sri Krishna commissioned us accordingly in this Holy Covenant and Oracle of His:

> *"He who suffers the sorrow of every creature,*
> *making each his own, him I hold the highest of all.*
> *A man should not hate any living creature.*
> *Let him be friendly and compassionate to all.*
> *Make your eyes more sensitive,*
> *your hearing more acute,*
> *and I will strengthen your arms!"*
>
> —*The Gita*

Sometime or the other, everyone of us might have extended a helping hand to someone in distress, put a smile on child's face, or, in extreme circumstances, may have even saved someone's life. And you would find that such acts beyond the call of duty give rise to a deep and rewarding feeling par excellence!

THE FOUR PERIODS OF LIFE

Righteous living is a condition precedent to God realization. Spiritual practices enjoin a strict code of conduct. Without moral scruple, spiritual progress would not at all be possible. And without spiritual progress, we can get nowhere in our bid to conquer death.

For the betterment of man, the rishis have codified life into Four *ashrams* or Periods. And these Four Periods serve the express purpose taking us step-by-step towards God— prepare us for the final moment when comes time for us to make peace with God.

As is evident in all of these periods, God consciousness

is the underlying theme in man's growth and development—
man's constant struggle to remain in ligature and vassal-
age with God. And laying the foundation to such a life of
idealism, here're a few cardinal principles cast in stone—
a prescriptive way of living ordained by the adroit rishis
themselves.

BRAHMACHARYA OR STUDENT LIFE

The first period is referred to as *brahmacharya* or student-
life. And literally translated, the word *brahmacharya* means
"divine or Brahman living." It is a period whereby the individual receives a thorough grounding in secular educa-
tion—is taught the arts and sciences.

But more importantly so too, he is also groomed mor-
ally, ethically and spiritually—nurtured in the admonition
of God's Holy Will. In short, it involves the holistic training and disciplining of one's mind, body and soul—molded
to a life of duty, purity and chastity.

GRIHASTHA OR HOUSEHOLDER

The second stage is called *grihastha* or life of a house-
holder. Its a time when one gets married and starts a family of his own—a period of procreation and perpetuation
of the human kind, as well as continuum of family values,
traditions, customs and beliefs.

Marriage is regarded as a sacred institution espoused by
the gods themselves. And as such, man and woman are
made for each other—a conjugal relationship ordained and
blessed by the Heavenly Father Himself. Therefore, whom
the gods put together let no man render asunder!

In the truest sense of the word, love is a not just a state
of mind. Much deeper and craftier than that, it involves also
the soul—man and woman opening up to the same Being.
And the fact that a couple can love each other in flesh and

blood finds its origin deep down within the spirit—love being transmitted through the medium of the body.

Marriage, therefore, is a divine play or *leela* of God. Wedlock involves two separate souls coming together for the sheer joy of love. And as a man tries to cleave and become one with his better half, so too the scriptures enjoin him to unite with the Holy Father in the end.

Hence the proverbial expression: "A man is incomplete without a wife." But so too is he without God. From God came man, and, in turn woman through man. And being inversely proportional then, upon returning to God man must first be in unanimity with his spouse before so cleaving with God.

And in this regards, here's a wonderful quote from the *Holy Bible*:

And Adam said:
"This is now bone of my bones,
and flesh of my flesh—
she shall be called woman
because she was taken out of man.
Therefore shall a man leave
his father and mother,
and shall cleave unto his wife;
and they shall be one flesh!"

God affords man this golden opportunity to unite himself with his wife in mind, body, heart and soul. And having successfully met this challenge, it would be so much easier for him to unite with God in the end—the one who loves him more than anyone else possibly could.

By coming together, a couple engages in an interplay or energy dynamics, whereby they stand a much better chance of survival than if left on their own. Bonded together, these two spiritual playmates form a partnership that has a lot to do with the evolution of their souls.

Instead of being of a sanctimonious nature only then, marriage is more of a sacramental value. Its a means of developing ones personality to its fullest potential both materially and spiritually—not to mention that it leads to a harmonious spousal relationship with no room for separation or divorce.

Let not your marriage that was created in heaven plummeth to hell!

RETIREMENT

In designing this great system, the rishis made the assumption that man would live a full life of a-hundred years. Therefore, the Four Periods were divided equally into Twenty-five years each. But seeing that life expectancy has somewhat tragically fallen, I shall incorporate these two last periods and call it the period of retirement.

After raising a family, the Founding Fathers held-out that a couple should finally look towards retirement. They should gradually give up all worldly possessions—free themselves from the bonds of attachment. And having already cleaved to each other, they should now together cleave to God.

Failing to adhere to these guiding principles, death could prove itself a very distasteful experience—deals man a deathly blow! And seeing that our hearts would be where our riches are, it is not difficult to understand why this becomes such an acute problem in our hands.

God does not condone the amassing of wealth all the days of our lives. After all, it is only a means to an end. Having met and served that purpose, it outlives its importance there afterwards. It must be voluntarily and gracefully relinquished in full satisfaction and contentment thereof.

Describing it as the period of *renunciation,* Sri Krishna in abjuration thereof urged mankind to give up everything —seek in finality the enviable goal and prize of his life. And here's a beautiful story that illustrates the importance and significance of renunciation:

Once a rich young man asked Jesus:
"Good master,
what shall I do
that I may inherit eternal life?"

And replying to him, Jesus reproached and admonished him by these very words of His:

"One thing thou lackest:
go thy way, sell whatsoever thou hast,
and give it to the poor
and thou shalt have treasures in heaven:
and come, take up thy cross,
and follow me."

And yet on another occasion the Lord Jesus is quoted as saying: "It's easier for a camel to enter a needle's eye than a rich man to enter the kingdom of God"—importing the meaning that, holding on in futility to ones wealth, precludes him entering God's Holy Kingdom.

Renunciation brings with it instant peace to the spirit of man—and so does too purity of conduct. And if we were to apply this doctrine in our lives, it will facilitate joyful acceptance of the final and most crucial separation of all—death. And given its inevitability, one would be ill advised not to be so prepared!

Abnegation also enables one to come to grips with this very emotional and traumatic experience. If nothing else, it lessens the pain associated with the pangs of separation and death. And for the fully enlightened person, it even renders him oblivious to any sufferings whatsoever as we would see later on.

What a beautiful and thoughtful system this is! From beginning to end, it is designed with this one lofty idea in mind: *How to make man god.* And as you can see, there's nothing the rishis think, say or do that God is not brought into play—made a party to. And in proposal of this sublimed way of life, they wove only salutary and godlike strands into the fabric of their beings!

A CLARIFICATION

It must not be misconstrued that Hinduism estops or forbids one enjoying life. This is a misnomer that indubitably needs clarification. As a matter-of-fact, Hinduism advocates four principal rewards subdivided as follows:

Dharma: Religious merits

Aartha: Acquisition of wealth

Kaama: Pleasure

Moksha: Emancipation

However, there are codes of conduct governing each of these pursuits that cannot be compromised. For instance, the acquisition of wealth must be by righteous and fair means only. And pleasure must be what's good and beneficial to one's health and spiritual well-being—fall within the ambits of religious tenets and principles.

And *moksha* (which in essence is the very topic of this book) concerns itself with how man finally detaches himself from everything and comes to the unitive knowledge—representing a stage of unwinding and preparation for the final experience.

HOW TO KNOW GOD

Tackling the Art of Living in a single chapter imposes a lot of restrictions. All I can do here is simply touch on some salient points pertaining thereto. And not withstanding any of it, I shall like to end this chapter with some wonderful thoughts in mind presented in a book *How to Know God* by Dr. Deepak Chopra.

We have just dealt with the Four *ashrams* or Periods of life. Chopra in turn came up with the Seven Stages one must be submerged in before so emerging to find God. And he presented his findings along the same lines as did the rishis, although from a slightly different perspective.

He brought to light the physiological and psychological changes one undergoes, putting to use his specialized knowledge and training as a medical doctor. And what is truly noteworthy here is how much *evolution* plays a part in man's struggle to reach the spiritual plateau of his life.

SPIRITUAL EVOLUTION

Getting connected to God does not happen overnight just like that. Rather than being a sudden flight atop the spiritual ladder, it entails following a prescribed Course or Art—undergoing a form of refinement even as gold is processed from its crude ore-state.

There is no magic formula or short-cut either. Knowing God involves a process phased-in over the years—a rising pattern or arc instead of a linear journey. It's an integrative approach, which, like the longest journey that begins with a single step, one must only be prepared to make a start. To have begun is to have the job half done.

Taking into account too my own life, I have seen what a riffraff it has been. Like a learning laboratory, the world is an environment of great experimentation. And in my endeavor to decipher everything, it took me nearly fifty years of trial and error to accomplish just that—a learning process still very much in progress today.

In real life, we've all got to do the *rumba*—undergo the

growing pains and motions of it all. And by so doing, I came to the conclusion that the means do not necessarily justify the end. For example, the more it seems one gets, the more he wants—seldom satisfied with what's allotted him.

Thus enslaved and imprisoned by my desires, I hit this discordant and dolorous note in my life. There came a time when my body could no longer keep up with the quickened pace. And approaching this crossroad, I felt no less a living dead—loss in my own vicious world.

Towards midstream, I discovered that the things which once appealed to me no longer did. Developing inside of me was this insipidness—the desire for worldly things beginning to wane. And though blessed with all the good things of life, I nonetheless found something vitally missing in mine—there was this gaping void or vacuum in my life!

But lucky for me, I have always been in the company of saints—monks in the likes of my guru. And following in their footsteps by surrendering my life to God, everything unholy abortively began to give—in abhorrence whereof, *abstinence* became the watchword in my life!

An avowed Aryan by heart, one day at the crack of dawn I began to internalize God's supreme presence— to accost myself en bloc all things extraneous or extrinsic to my spiritual development.

Having thus trimmed myself of this sort of corpulence, I watched the unfolding of my true higher innerself. I suddenly found the urge to relive the life of the ancient rishis. Albeit an abridged version of theirs, I grew in the strength of character and resolve.

In the ensuing process, an intervening closeness fostered itself between me, the monks, the rishis and God—my newfound friends I so much longed to be with. And the closer I got to them, the better it felt inside—an evolution once initiated works wonders in my life.

Consequentially, I felt now cushioned and upheld by these greater forces—the resultant birth of a new me. And with this spiritual transformation and metamorphosis happening all around me, I became inundated with many wonderful divine encounters and experiences—having a taste of which made me realize what a wonderful world this is.

It's a world though that is in a constant state of flux. As a matter-of-fact, the cosmos is simply structured that way— whereby *change* or *evolution* is the law. And as there's nothing in all of this universe that remains absolutely static, man in maturation thereof finds himself in a position where he simply just cannot afford not to evolve—more so being the most complex and involute creation of all.

Speaking of change, geriatric or growing old is not all bad news after all. As we know only too well, wisdom dawns with age. And being that man is as old as he thinks, dotage and senility are just a state of mind—man progressively evolving as he goes through the grooming processes of life. And the older he gets, the wiser he becomes.

But quite apart from these spiritual and evolutionary changes, getting to know God also involves specific biological transformations. And by nature of our superior human birth, we come specially equipped to handle these involved systemic reflex reactions—bringing into play the ingenuity of the brain, the mind, and God all reacting in this supreme cause of action: *Man in the making of a god.*

It has been pointed out, however, that if we do not experience these changes it is because some parts of our brains remain totally dormant. Spiritual awakening, as it is rightfully termed, reminds me of a story often told in India. It's an allegory of a child prince who was kidnapped by robbers.

Raised among bandits, he completely adopted to their style of life—forgot his early life and origin. Now a grown man, he was discovered by an emissary of the king. Recognizing him, he embraced and addressed him as "Your Highness." But the bandit repeatedly shoved him away, persistent as he was.

Then he began to remind the prince of his childhood days. Slowly but surely, scenes of his early palace life were coming back to him. "I am not a bandit," he eventually declared. "Just that I forgot who I was." And upon returning to his kingdom, he took up his rightful inheritance. And that's how it is to be awakened to one's true inner divineness.

After enjoying a meteoric rise to fame, Chopra masterfully delineated the Seven Stages one undergoes before he gets to know God—a process that hinges on the spiritual, evolutionary and biological changes alluded to above. And in a moment, I shall compress them in a nutshell for you.

Covered in the following section are the traits that characterise each stage. And Stage One, for example, represents man's breaking off point from his primitive animal ancestry—tendencies that progressively get wiped out as one ascends the spiritual ladder.

And fortunately enough, each ensuing stage takes us higher and higher—closer and closer to God. But for those of us who choose not to migrate upwards, we get stuck at this base or primary level all our lives. The choice of getting to know God is ours—to be or not to be a god!

STAGE ONE: FIGHT OR FLIGHT RESPONSE

At the basic or fundamental level of life is survival—the biological and inborn instinct inherited from our animal counterparts. And what else could it be but our defense mechanism and preparedness to meet external endangerment in the form predators and other suchlike threats.

A good example of this reflex action is the way we begrudgingly guard and protect the young, even as animals do. Not wanting anything untoward happening to them, men-turned-daredevils react with much belligerence and pugnacity. No different from werewolves, these querulous and brutish Homo Sapiens bombastically boast of their vain physical prowess and Herculean strength—apply the truculent harum-scarum techniques in life.

Trying to outfox one another, the Darwinism evolutionary theory of *survival of the fittest* holds particularly true here—man living in a truly draconian world that at times demands the show of courage in face of adversities.

But in our struggle to survive, we must not do so at the expense of other living things. Gratuitously and opulently has the Good Lord provided a plethora of vegetation on which all can comfortably survive—the most delectable herbs, grains, fruits, diary products. And as such, there's absolutely no need or cause to go beyond this just in order to satisfy our insatiable appetite and craving thereto.

Seeking not to incriminate anyone, it is considered a hideous sin (venial and pardonable I trust) if we were to do the unspeakable—kill. But unthinkable as it is, the errant man often enough does—knowing fully well that it is an act of grave sacrilege as far as the Merciful Lord is concerned.

Adjudged the best of connoisseurs, the conscionable rishis rightly praised *vegetarianism*—the victuals and ambrosia fit for the gods. They refuse to let their entrails become graveyards—a promulgation that finds fulfillment in the *Holy Bible*. Here's this remarkable statement presented verbatim:

32 ❖ *The Joys of Death*

> *"Behold! I have given you*
> *every herb bearing seed*
> *which is upon the face of all the earth,*
> *and every tree—*
> *to you it shall be for meat."*
>
> —*The Bible*

At this initial stage of the game, the egregious and God-forsaken individual is in a languishing mode—resulting in him having just a remote chance of getting to know God. And due to this lassitude and lethargy overshadowing him, his life is encumbered with many ignoble qualities—all on account of his own ineptitude, voracity and incredulous nature.

Such boisterous, culpable and cavilmen (men of evil propensities) who could care less about their spiritual growth get stagnated at this contemptible level—complaining, ranting and raving over every conceivable little thing. And suffering too from an abject or servile lack of spirit, these impecunious and sinister folks take for granted whatever life has to offer them—dwell in a constant state of purgatory and pandemonium.

Their eccentric and portentous behavior is of such that when they speak even, they are of such mordacious and caustic tongues. Their vituperative and highfalutin language could catapult and pierce your heart like bullets shot at you. Hailed an act of notoriety, such blabbermouth and cantankerous men could easily incriminate their least suspecting fellow compatriots even—nay their very own flesh and blood!

These grotesque, whimsical and magniloquent men are even capable of making inflammatory statements against their very own Benefactor. Who were those libidinous characters that performed the dastardly and pusillanimous act of nailing to the cross our Beloved Jesus Christ? Weren't they inhumane men that gyrate at the low, preparatory level of Stage One?

Such depraved, malevolent and malignant men (recreant and recalcitrant losers) are betwixt and between man and his animal descendants. Their recriminating and diabolical inclinations are of such that you would want to think of Stage One as being no more a cat-and-dog life—man's struggle to keep body and soul together!

And as such, there is a forlorn cry and acute separation from God. Frail and peevish to begin with, the lives of these hapless ones are further impeded or tormented by this rather simplistic notion of theirs: They think of themselves as complete nonentities stranded on the vast expanse of the cosmos.

And suffering too from inertia and ignominy, these enfeebled and impoverished ones are considered lost souls. Constantly governed by trepidation and fear, they, in dire need thereof, concern themselves only with the bare nitty-gritty of life—not in any way different from what animals do where their sustenance is concerned.

STAGE TWO: REACTIVE RESPONSE

Fearing the worst then, Stage One can be seen in light where the debutant or neophyte relies on his base instincts to survive and dominate his environment. Being unable to integrate and take up his rightful place in God's Holy Ethos or Mosaic, the baneful one is barred from making that all-important Providential connection.

And vegetating like this, he is branded an unworthy inhabitant in the eyes of God. Unfortunately, he isolates himself by choosing to be a desolate and lonely soul—an outcaste more dead than alive. He simply does not rise to the challenge—meet the high standard expected of him.

It is rather unfortunate that these passive and pedantic

individuals cannot mobilize and make their lives good, viable propositions—put to use the enormous influences available to them. And having just emerged from Stage One, there's this rabid, lingering feeling of apprehension still lurking over their heads, especially where having to trust God and the universe are concerned.

Cynical to begin with, what a pathetic and lamentable stage to be in also! And seeing there's a prevailing tendency for him to find something tangible to hold on to, the god-less one responds by creating a monster in form of his own quisling ego. And having this axe to grind, the ego, brought out center stage, makes him act with such impetuosity and turpitude—oblivious to the pains and sufferings of all others.

But with their basic needs met and fears subsided in the latter part of Stage Two, there now exits at this Reactive Response Stage a real potential to know God. Granted a bit of impunity, they do not feel so much traumatized, sequestered and alienated from God anymore—man in his forward march and thrust towards God.

At the latter part of Stage Two, there's the onset of some sort of inner growth and expansion happening in the lives of these once totally naïve ones. Thus, their heathen and suspicious nature are being gradually replaced by more God-fearing ways. They feel that they can do much more now than just merely survive.

But still very much incapacitated and stigmatized, they find that they could fortify their positions by initiating and befriending the Divine. And regarded as the most conventional ways to connect to God, they discover that when they pray they actually get what they want.

STAGE THREE: RESTFUL AWARENESS RESPONSE

And even though the individual has been through the first

couple tentative stages, he is still by and large considered a novice. Oscillating back and forth, he is held at limbo here—still much in a torpid state of hibernation where alignment with God and his soul are concerned.

However, it's not much of a predicament (something to quibble over) since he is on the verge of making a major breakthrough here. There's a ray of hope and proffer for help—the pointing of the mind towards the powerful inner-man he is. And this impalpably makes Stage Three the commencement of an inward journey. It clearly ushers in a newfound source of strength—the kindling of this inner fire from deep within.

No longer showing signs of diffidence or a lackadaisical attitude, the individual begins to experience something meaningful happening to him: An evolution has taken place near their hearts—the end result being that their nascent selves are blossoming beyond the point of mediocrity.

Introspectively delving deeper and deeper, their inner-world and lines of communications begin to open up. And since real strength begins with the intangible anchored deep down within the spirit, tapping even slightly into the realm of the Self adds a totally new dimension to one's life.

Realizing that he is no longer alone, there's also the prevalence of a larger and greater force drawing nigh, which is nonesuch but God. And this Stage of Restful Awareness typifies a significant turning point in ones life—the crossroad where he begins to gravitate closer and closer towards God.

Hitherto mellow and plaintive, the individual is now more contrite, remorseful, penitent, compunctious. And desperately seeking to curb his incorrigible ways, he makes a deliberate effort in the show of retribution and restitution. Not as sordid and secular anymore, rudimentary principles begin to make way for more elevated and sanctifying ways.

STAGE FOUR: INTUITIVE RESPONSE

Here a totally new person is in the making. As if by the touch of an Exorcist, there's the emergence of a strong, multi-dimensional genius of a man. Having been spiritually awakened, he now speedily evolves beyond the threshold of the impecunious and pauperized five-sensory man he once was.

Expanding upon his five-sensory capacity, his garnering of the power of *intuition* now leads him in full cry to the discovery of his real higher Self—his resourceful *soul-force-field* which is a template or dynamo of vast power and intelligence.

Becoming aligned thereto, man taps into a higher frequency or mode of energy current running through his body. And having thus drank from this infinite reservoir, his life begins to resonate with sheer dynamism and power.

With this renewed vitality comes an enraptured feeling of inward peace and tranquility, infiltrating and making its way deeper and deeper into the being of man. Thus intuitively seeking the Higher Self, it results in the dawn of a new you—a discovery, once made, enables man to fly through space and time.

All of a sudden his inner-world has come alive—man in communication with his true divine mystical Self. And consequentially, he finds himself in a position where he can now comprehend the intricacies of the Mother of the Universe—she who patiently awaits the opportunity to unfold her cherished secrets unto him.

And from this vantage point, man gets real fascinated with life. Discovering that his ego was betraying him all along, he no longer wants to have anything to do with it either. Convinced that only he knows what's best for him, the individual is now more decisive and forthright in everything he says and does.

Full of synergism, he intuits that too many things are happening to him that could no longer be explained using the same old yardstick, line of reasoning and value systems. And with this sweeping, gushing wave of spiritual deluge, he boldly enters hitherto uncharted territories. His deep inner-gut-feelings, voice of conscience and intuition are all sensational insights and flashes across from the Universal Mind of God.

Upheld by this greater force, there's nothing in all of this world that could shake him any longer. And having thus made breaking contact with all residual effects of blemishes, guilt and shame, man is finally absolved of all sins—in exoneration whereof he plunges deeper and deeper into the abode of his creative Self and God overall.

STAGE FIVE: THE CREATIVE RESPONSE

Intuition begets *creativity* that in turn begets ones true multi-sensory self—proving again that man is very much beyond the limitations of his five-senses. And for the lack of a better word, *multi-sensory* refers to anything above and beyond the collective forces of the five senses—sight, smell, taste, hearing, and touch.

Therefore, in addition to the five senses, man can come to rely on his other adjunct and auxiliary powers—amplify and make good his more inordinate *intuitive* and *creative* faculties. And having thus composed oneself, he can now be rightly said to be multi-sensory in nature.

Risen to the pinnacle of mental fortitude, a typical example of a true multi-sensory individual was the resilient Gandhi. Though of a fragile mortal coil, his charismatic and visionary leadership saw the mighty British Empire yielding to his relentless cry for freedom and liberty. A born redeemer, the protagonist Gandhi even died a martyr!

Godsend and Great White Hope of his people, he was operating at an optimum energy level running through his being. And everything else being equal, his power of *intuition* and *creativity* bore testimony to his great insights and hunches—messages emitted from his most blessed *soul-force-field*.

As his creative ingenuity surges forth, man is joined in this cooperative enterprise with the Maker—become a fitting instrument in the Hands of God. Being also the Prototype He is, God is now in full control of the person's life—in alignment whereof man's individuality is now sunk into the greater identity with God.

Coming under the influence of the Creator, he feels himself truly blessed. Instead of merely relying on his *soul-force-field*, his authentic empowerment can now be traced to *God-force-field* as well—wherefore, somewhere along the line he manages to break loose and is home free at last.

Swept and brought here by this deep current, he is now whom he wants to be, doing what he always wanted to do. He feels reassured that amidst the vicissitudes of life, God has been keeping a watchful eye over him. And instead of just merely holding his hands, he is now being carried by God.

STAGE SIX: THE VISIONARY RESPONSE

Fully purged of all delinquencies and deficiencies, one now embraces a life of vast expansion that practically spans the world. Having grown so much in the strength of character, he is now on the verge of giving up all material possessions—in exchange for which he elects an introspective life of contemplative solitude.

And in compliance thereof, the lionhearted Gandhi took

the oath of perpetual poverty—not to mention also renunciation and celibacy. Garbed in tattered rags, this half-naked fakir became the instrument of immense power—the repertoire of such spiritual dynamism gained only through the practice of continence.

And simultaneously taking place here also is an alarming array of physiological transformations—resulting in the brain getting extremely coherent. And given time, the intensification of it leads to the development of many wonderful visionary responses—a God-consciousness that leaves the nervous system totally charmed and overwhelmed.

Stage Six then represents another good reason why a spiritually awakened man can be termed multi-sensory. According to the science of Iridology, one's vision (the spiritual third-eye of wisdom) becomes fully protruded. No longer clouded over by delusion, the individual envisions God and him are together now—in visualization whereof his mind becomes fully attuned to the Cosmic Mind.

Enjoying a sweet intimacy with God, he feels no more separated from Him—in conjunction whereof he sees God in all, and all in God. Thus the individual considers himself having made a quantum leap—enters a stage where not even miracles are impossible anymore.

And being among her choicest sons and daughters, the Mother has finally unveiled all her long-held secrets unto him. Having seen the Plan of God as it relates to him both personally and universally, man is on the brink of being joined to His Maker—is in the process of becoming a god himself.

Filled with piety, benevolence and compassion, his heart at this stage is brimming over with the milk of human love—feels the urge to devote his entire life to the selfless service of his lesser unfortunate brethren. But at times, the

suffering proves too much for his bleeding, aching heart—
makes him want to escape this world altogether.

Wasn't this the very same way the down-to-earth Gandhi and commiserative Buddha felt too, which, in case of
the latter, led to his attainment of *nirvana?* And so it is too
with all other saintly personalities before and after them—
men who felt that the only work of interest to them is
amelioration of the lot of the downtrodden.

And so long as there is a single individual in need of the
Saving Grace of God, these altruistic personalities (philan-
thropists) would not rest in peace. As far as they are concerned, serving deserving mankind is verily serving God.
Friends of all the world, they seek to return good for evil—
not the other way around.

STAGE SEVEN: THE SACRED RESPONSE

In quixotry then, Stage Seven represents closing of the last
minuscule gap between the soul of man and God. There
are no further choices to make, as all hurdles are overcome
and boundaries crossed. There's no further need for
prayers even—though it is recommended until our dying
day.

The sage at this stage no longer identifies himself personally as Gandhi. He is now the affable Christ in him. As
far as man is concerned, spiritual evolution is complete.
Having merged in the God he reveres, that tiny point is
finally expanded into infinitude. Man in rapidity now di-
vulges himself into the god he's destined to become.

There is now no distinguishing between himself and
God, for in unity all separation ends. Being the sole purpose of the evolutionary process, the soul eventually re-
turns to its immortal, blissful and timeless state— surren-
ders or lapses into God's Holy Trust and Safekeeping.

Representing man's quest for liberation and emanci-

pation, *nirvana* is that coveted state one begrudgingly
strives for. Having undergone this spiritual transmutation
or metamorphosis, *nirvana* is undoubtedly that pertinent
state where the soul of man shines through and reaches
oneness with God.

The human experience is a journey towards wholeness
and perfection—a destiny that awaits each and everyone
of us if we so choose. And with the much recent publicity
and literary work undertaken in this area of endeavor, an
exciting time has come of age—an era of spiritual resur-
gence.

One of the greatest spiritual masters of our times Srimat
Swami Pranavanandaji Maharaj proclaimed it the Golden
Age: "A time for universal awakening, universal unification,
universal synthesis, universal emancipation—men in their
collective thrust towards Godhood."

Most of what is presented here in this book shall fluctu-
ate back-and-forth the latter stages, with Stage Seven taking precedence over all the rest. And having now presented you with this preamble, you could imagine the
wealth of knowledge lying in store here for you.

❖ *Three* ❖

Mind Above Matter

A BACKGROUND NOTE

The unprecedented and pristine glory that is India is today being disseminated worldwide. Thanks to brilliant minds in the likes of His Holiness Maharshi Mahesh Yogi and Dr. Deepak Chopra—both of whose insightful thinking have earned them the deepest respect and admiration.

And as you travel into the world of the rishis, you are left with the overwhelming feeling that you have been to a place that has never been more fully explored. After all its India where first arose the doctrines of the Immortality of the Soul, Karma and Reincarnation.

Compiled in the Vedas, these findings were recorded in Sanskrit believed to be man's first language ever. And not only are they the oldest, but also the most important scriptures of the Hindus. Superfluous and voluminous in nature, they represent the very frontier of knowledge—incorporate man's cumulative archaic wisdom of yore.

And etymologically speaking, the word Veda is a derivative of the Sanskrit word *vid* meaning "to know." And not only do the Vedas portray Hindus in-depth knowledge of the much sophisticated human body, but they also incorporate their comprehension of things generally—give a conspectus account of all there is to know.

The Vedas are the revealed scriptures of the Hindus—the eternal word or divine dispensation handed down from God to humanity. In short, orthodox Hindus recognize in them the origin of their Faith and the highest written authority there is. In other words, they are encyclopedic storehouses or archives outlining all of the Physical and Metaphysical laws there are—a consortium if you will.

And in order to better appreciate the impact Vedic knowledge and philosophy may have had on our lives, let's look at just this one exemplification or archetype thereof—the *mind/body connection.* By no means anachronistic in any may, it has captivated much attention upon its introduction into the Western society.

THE MIND/BODY CONNECTION

One of the guiding principles of Ayurveda (considered as a supplement of the *Atharvaveda*) is that the *mind* exerts the deepest influence over the body. And as you would see later on, mind-control is of paramount importance in our quest to defeat this most unconquerable opponent and adversary of all—death.

The preeminent Vedic seers mastered this most ancient Art and Technique. And to such an incredible degree they were adept to mind-control that they brought about near miraculous changes to their health and spiritual wellbeing.

Grown inured thereof, these undaunted rishis deliberately subjugated themselves to all manner of extraneous and painstaking exercises. And to demonstrate their astringent efforts thereto, below is a sampling of a few valiant and mind-boggling acts of theirs—some that demanded the show of great chivalry, grit and willpower that could literally take your breath away:

Ghastly holding their breath for unusually long periods of time.

Voluntarily reducing their heart rates to near zero.
Buried for days six feet underground in enclosed boxes.

With all of our God given abilities and superior biochemical infrastructure, man is the only creature on earth that can change his biology by the way he thinks and feels—by his mere thoughts in other words. And not realizing that we are gifted as such, we tend to ignore this all important aspect of our human traits.

The problem is that by following the status quo we have all programed our subconscious minds with the idea that we are going to grow old, get sick and fall prey to death—send the wrong messages and signals to our bodies. And unsurprisingly so, its no surprise we suffer the full consequences of our ill-fated thoughts.

It is an axiomatic or proverbial truth that one gets out of life what one comes to expect from it. It's all in our heads so-to-speak—the way we think and program our subconscious minds. And as far as the rishis were concerned, they had their priorities quite in order. Authors or masters of their own destinies, for them it was mind above matter—and not the other way around.

OUR TRUE MENTAL CAPACITY

A major breakthrough in the dissemination of the prodigious feats of the rishis was made by the much celebrated author Deepak Chopra. He was among the first to have convincingly demonstrated the efficacy of *mind/body* techniques in solving health related problems based on the application of Ayurveda—affording man an opportunity to choose *perfect health* for himself.

Taken an affront and contortion thereto, most reputable medical journals once looked at this proposition as a taboo or laughing matter—ridicule the idea that sickness and health might be dependent on something as shadowy as one's mind.

Before his work was published, the *mind/body* connection was merely taken for granted. Mind and body were separated by an "old thick wall." As a matter-of-fact, the mind was seen as a ghost and the body a machine—totally separated as far as modern medicine was concerned.

But much to the dismay of Western thinking, we all know only too well how much our mind (and attitude in general) impact upon us. And it took a mastermind in the person of Deepak Chopra to prove us wrong—speaking of which here's this brilliant interposition of his:

"But now that would change. The mind/body connection is real and here's the proof! A flood of messenger molecules course through the blood stream, transforming our most intimate thoughts, emotions, beliefs, prejudices, wishes, dreams and fears into physical realities. Mind turns into matter not at the higher point of a magical act but at the ordinary business of the body's fifty trillion cells.

You cannot experience the faintest mood without your heart cells sharing it—and at the same time your lungs, kidneys, stomach, intestine. Our intelligence cannot be a ghost in a machine because the machine is in itself intelligent—and that means it isn't merely a machine after all.

Science has made it clear that we are physical machines that have somehow learnt to think—when in fact we are 'thoughts' that have created physical machines. I think this is the crowning discovery of the twentieth century medicine"—wrote Dr. Chopra.

MIND ABOVE MATTER

We have seen that people who keep themselves busy are known to have above average health. Whereas, those who worry excessively are more prone and susceptible to the ravages of diseases—having of course much to do with the way they think.

We can appreciate here also the value of *breakthrough thinking*, which is a unique form of problem solving. It's a process whereby you raise your expectations much higher than anyone else believes possible. And then you look next for ways and means to make your dream come true.

Anything in your body can be changed by the flick of an intention. And how much more powerful wouldn't it be if one were to employ a process as powerful as this! The mind indubitably has a very penetrating effect on our entire being. But now it's a foregone conclusion and scientifically proven fact.

REMISSION OF DISEASES

It is the mind what directs us where to go and what to do, which in turn eventually leads us on to health, sickness and death. And not only in the waking, but also in the dream state the mind has a very strong influence over the body— the placebo effect being a case in point.

If, for example, one were to dream he's being attacked by a ferocious animal, there would be a series of predictable, symptomatic reactions: The adrenaline gets going, blood pressure sours, heart palpitates, breathing accelerates, perspiration trickles. There exists this semblance of events as if in a real life situation.

If then during the dream state the mind has such a far-reaching effect on our bodies, what greater influence wouldn't it have in the conscious waking state—a time when the body and mind are at their optimum operating capacity?

By being positive, unimaginative healing power can be unleashed from within. And being itself a form of driving light, the human machinery can be made to run at an optimum level—the frequency of which is directly proportional to the thoughts one harbors.

From a medical and technical point of view, emotional impulses produce currents of energy with varying degrees or levels of frequencies. And take *love* as an example! It can be shown any day that it produces a much higher energy frequency than would malevolence, jealousy or malice.

Abounding or teeming with energy, a loving and kindhearted person is one full of zest and vitality—someone who enjoys overall better health. And on the other hand you have your depressing and boring counterpart who not only does harm to himself but also devour your much vital energy. There's absolutely no power at all in negativity and pessimism.

Negative stimuli such as anger and bitterness release toxins that lower our resistance; whereas positive ones such as patience and forgiveness protect and heal. And in order that the body may remain healthy, the mind must be first wooed and made a friend. A healthy mind in a health body is what it takes.

It has been shown in medical studies too that if a disease is not too far advanced, changing the way we think can bring about a reversion or remission of the process. And this makes it imperative for us to have a total shift in perspective—develop a new and better outlook to life.

And although it's beyond the scope of this book, I feel it is somewhat mandatory to make even passing comments on this landmark medical discovery. Chopra cited in one of his books incidences where a significant number of patients, recovery defied all medical interpretations. And in one such study, doctors made it a point to look at terminally ill patients.

Now whether these patients had contracted deadly diseases, or, were otherwise involved in near fatal accidents, were totally irrelevant. What matters most was the fact that they were all seriously ill and beyond the point of recovery. In fact, all medical help was hopelessly ruled out.

But what they discovered was that many of these patients astonishingly got up and literally walked away from it all. And here's now a medical insider offering perhaps the most probable scientific explanation of all. And its one too that coincides with what the rishis were saying all along—the only difference being that Chopra has now quantified and affixed a label to it called *quantum healing*.

QUANTUM HEALING

From a purely scientific point of view, the body cures diseases by utilizing its own built-in mechanism traced to the most creative level of ones awareness—a phenomenon that involves the mind above anything else.

Masterminding the excavation and unearthing of this long buried or hidden secret, Chopra marveled and stunned the medical world with the exposition of his profound *Theory of Quantum Healing*—the ability of ones mode of consciousness (the mind) to spontaneously correct the mistakes in another mode of consciousness (the body). And in elucidation thereof, he elaborated as follows:

"To comprehend how this is made possible, we have to delve deep into the human body. In Ayurveda, the physical body is the gateway to what I shall like to refer to as the Quantum Mechanical Human Body.

Physics informs us that the basic fabric of nature lies at the quantum level, far beyond atoms and molecules. Defined as the basic unit of matter or energy, a quantum is from 10,000 to 100,000,000 times smaller than the smallest atom known to man.

At this infinitesimal level, matter and energy become

interchangeable. Quanta, really speaking, are small discrete packets into which energy are subdivided. And they in turn are made up of invisible vibrations—ghosts of energy waiting to take physical form.

Ayurveda purports that the same is also true of the human body. It first takes on the form of intense but invisible vibrations called 'quantum fluctuations,' then proceeding next to coalesce into pulses of energy and particles of matter."

Thus Chopra went on to show that illness stems from distortions of the patterns of the quantum vibrations holding the body intact. And seeing that at the quantum level is found the seat of intelligence, by contacting it one can bring about instantaneous changes to the physical body.

And realizing that it is the mind what directs the body towards sickness and health, manipulating or maneuvering the mind could have beneficial effects. And this can result in the Quantum Mechanical Human Body being exploited to effect a change for the better—one too that is far more effective than drug, diet or exercise.

Freedom from sickness depends upon us contacting our awareness, bringing it into balance, and extending that balance to the body—a process whereby our lives can be ultimately influenced, shaped and extended without interference from sickness, old age and death.

CONTACTING OUR AWARENESS

And Chopra further explained that: "There exists in every person a place that is free from disease, never feels pain, cannot age or die. And when you go to that place, limitations we accept cease to exist—is no longer even entertained as a possibility. And this place is called 'Perfect Health'."

Long before modern medicine discovered the *mind-*

body connection, the incredulous rishis mastered it. They developed this inner technology that operates from the most inveterate level of ones awareness. And that's not all! They even taught us the technique how to get there—how to transcend and go quite beyond the mask of this physical sheet.

This topic shall be dealt with in all its glory under the section dealing with "Transcendental Meditation." And presented in all its exclusivity, it shall represent invitation to a Higher Reality—an exceptionally pivotal discovery in it's own right.

A SIMILAR ATTEMPT

I have given you here just a little glimpse of the Vedic contribution to the world of medicine—one that holds much promise even in today's world. And a similar sincere attempt is hereby made to bring out the Vedic Thoughts and Philosophy on life's most insidious and mind-boggling question—death.

Born and educated in the West and having Indian Hindu ancestry, I am in a quite unique position to bring out the best of both worlds. And without meaning to sound facetious in any way, I trust that you would find this masterful treatise quite authoritative and revealing.

I unreservedly make this solemn declaration that none of this is of my own doing. The ideas in this book took birth long before I did. All that I have done is to assimilate the facts and present my dissertation before you—act as a medium through the instrumentality of God.

✽ *Part Two* ✽

THE UNIVERSALITY THEORIES

Objectives

Before commencement of our discussions on the body, soul and death, we shall set out to achieve in this section the following statements of objectives:

The Law of Dharma
First we shall look at the Great Design of this marvelous universe we somehow strangely find ourselves in. And then we shall establish the *Universal Soul Theory*.

Where Science Stops the Vedas Begin
In this chapter we will examine the reality of the world— one espoused by the Holy Vedas and rishis to be delusive in nature.

The Law of Karma and Reincarnation
And finally we shall undertake a quick survey of these two underlying, cornerstone principles upon which we intend to build our ensuing discussions.

❋ Four ❋

The Law of Dharma

THE RIGHT ORDER OF THE COSMOS

*"I am the beginning,
the middle, and end of creation.
I am the origin, the sustainer.
and Lord of the three worlds."*

—Sri Krishna

COSMIC INTELLIGENCE

GIVEN a nuance of meaning, the word *dharma* is defined as that which sustains the individual and the world—the aggregate of all the laws and governing principles of the cosmos. Put differently, *dharma* determines the right course and order of the universe—a milieu or environ fully imbibed with sheer intelligence.

After creating the universe, God did not have to infuse it with the known-how to operate itself. That intelligence was there, built-in right from the very beginning. Originating from God, how could it be anything other than a great degree of sophistication—a universe that is supremely and positively charged with a glut of energy!

Thus inspired and convinced, scientists have coined a very beautiful and an all-encompassing phrase to define this widespread, intensified form of energy—referred to it as the *cosmic dance of energy*. And stop to think of it, the cosmogony is an energy-galore all by itself.

BODY COMPLEXITY

This vast degree of intelligence permeates everything starting with the tiniest cell down to the huge cosmos itself. This is one of the major discoveries of the rishis and seers of India. They found the body to be a superficial layer empowered by millions of years of intelligence—and one too that is grounded in a quantum reality.

Let's look at the intricate manner in which the minute cells of our bodies operate. Take for instance when one is wounded. It is shown in medical studies that the blood cells rush to the wounded site and immediately commence to form a clot. And to begin with, their destination was not randomly determined. They know exactly where to go and what to do once they get there.

The clotting mechanism is an incredibly complex reaction so much so that if it fails the medical world is at a loss to duplicate it. And though manmade drugs can be administered to replace the missing clotting factors, they would not be as effective as the ones produced by the human body—drugs that are miraculously always of the right dosage with no side-effects.

The intelligence of the human body is even more startling when looked at from its DNA perspective—the most stable chemical component in our bodies. DNA insures that inherent genetic traits from our parents get transferred to us intact, which we in turn preserve and pass on to our children.

Speaking about a blueprint, it is unbelievable that our bodies possess such supra-intelligence even at the cellular level, encoded therein in those super microchips of ours. And if at this insignificant level is possessed such remarkable intelligence, then how much more wouldn't it be at the human level—and for that matter the elephantine level of the macrocosm?

HIGHLY REGULATED COSMOS

Behold the complexity and incomprehensibly wondrous nature of this commodious conglomerate—this abysmal, grandiose and cyclopean colossus of ours! And behold too the pageantry, the panoramic spectacle and pre- ponderance of such esthetic beauty—a physiognomy sec- ond to none!

You mean this gamut or gargantuan expanse happened purely by chance—the world simply fell into place by acci- dent just like that! But how could this be? Look around and take notice! Take the sun for example. It sustains trillions of lives here on earth. And without it no life would be possible at all.

Though separated by a void of 93 million miles, around it revolves the earth, held in orbit by gravity. And just half of a billionth of the sun's energy (a little trickle or drib- ble of it) reaches our planet, which, if efficiently har- nessed, could surprisingly meet the needs of modern day society worldwide with power to spare.

Could you imagine the engineering feat and crafts- manship involved putting all of this together! And just as if by some magical act, it even runs by itself—ever so self- generating, self-replenishing, self-driven. Unlike any man- made gadgets, there's never the need for fuel, repairs, nor replacement of worn-out parts. And it comes also with an ironclad guarantee.

And this is not only applicable to the sun! The earth, the moon, the firmament, the sky with its galaxy of stars, as well as the host of all other natural wonders of the world intrinsically follow the same guiding principle— reaching unto the very heights of sophistication I sup- pose.

SOVEREIGNTY OF GOD

There's this natural order and symmetry in the cosmos—everything congruently coming together with such precision and exactitude. It's an unthinkable imbrication that is highly regulated and automatic—voluntarily follow the correct sequence without the need of a conscious mind to direct it.

In his wisdom, Maharshi Mahesh Yogi also view the world in the same light: "The galaxies do not just run about here and there at random. There is an order in creation. And without the fundamental value of intelligence, all of this order and growth would not be found. Order seems to be evident when viewed as a whole. Intelligence is seen to work systematically throughout nature in a set-pattern. They seem to obey a regularity—a constancy that is quite in harmony and unison with one another."

The cosmos works by itself to direct and change itself—find a way to accomplish everything effortlessly and efficiently. And this steady outpouring of energy and intelligence proclaims not the unconscious throbbing of a soulless machine, but the stupendous effort of an all-knowing spirit. It can't be that it makes its rounds willy-nilly just like that.

These natural laws under which the universe operates purport a divine governance, sovereignty and theocracy. There has to be someone at helm of it all. And that someone could be nonesuch but the Theistic and Patriarchal Father Himself.

God is another name for this illimitable, unquantifiable, inexhaustible spiritedness and power—God in his Cosmological Hiding Place! And His supremacy is so much immanent that we only have to open our eyes and take notice.

And having ascribed or designated the world as such, we find that the proponents of *pantheism* would be elated hearing this: It's a philosophy that upholds the belief that God and the universe are identical. The world bears an id that matches that of the Demiurge Father.

In corroboration thereto, we find the Omniscient Lord Sri Krishna's ratification quite interesting. Without any circumlocution, He provided us this remarkable exegesis whereby He forthrightly proclaimed Himself as being supremely manifested in all things there are—a universe that is meticulously orchestrated by no one else but Him:

> *"The womb of all beings,*
> *I am the birth of this cosmos,*
> *and its dissolution too.*
> *I am the beginning, the middle,*
> *and the end of creation—*
> *the origin, sustainer*
> *and Lord of the three worlds.*
> *I am the radiant sun among light-givers,*
> *and the moon among the stars.*
> *Know me as the divine seed of everything.*
> *Nothing animate or inanimate exists without me.*
> *There's no limit to my manifestations,*
> *nor can they be numbered too.*
> *And what I have described to you*
> *are but few of my countless forms.*
> *But what need have you, Arjuna,*
> *to know of this huge variety?*
> *Know ye that only one atom of mine*
> *sustains the entire universe!"*

—*The Gita*

The Lord categorically and unequivocally declared that: "He is the origin, the divine seed, the womb, the sun, the moon, the earth, the life-span, death—the one who sustains all the worlds. Verily, there's no limit to His divine manifestations, nor can they be numbered too."

As if the remiss Arjuna should have known better, the Lord remonstrated him with the mentioning of these words: "What need have you to know of this huge variety? Though magnificent and countless in number, whatever you see represents only a tiny fraction of my power and glory. Just one atom of mine sustains this entire conglomerate."

COLLECTIVE CONSCIOUSNESS

The Theory of Everything

"I feel myself so much a part of all life
that I am not in the least concerned
with the beginning or the end
of the concrete existence of any particular person
in this unending stream."

—Einstein

"A part of all life in this unending stream!" This statement certainly connotes or gives the impression that we are all somehow bonded together. And that being the case then, why should we be concerned with the concrete existence of any one particular individual only, asked a genius like Einstein.

But this viewpoint is now a foregone conclusion. And building further on our hypothesis, we are now ready to make another projection. It can be shown that there's this intricate interconnectedness among all of nature—a *collective or macro-consciousness.*

And in approaching the topic, let's start by looking at the famous mathematical formula known as *Bell's Theorem*—a hypothesis suggestive of the fact that all events of this non-localized cosmos are generally interconnected.

And the same was supported too by British physicist David Bohm in his theory pertaining to the *invisible field.*

Just as an individual mental frame of mind can be altered to bring about remission of diseases, similarly there's nothing to prevent the process happening externally too. It can be shown that what one individual does affect another—emphasizing the fact that reality is collectively shared.

Most advanced thinkers in the field of Physics today do support the *collective consciousness hypothesis*—a supposition that explains the singleness or oneness of the universe. And Sir James Jeans aptly puts it this way: "In the deeper reality beyond space and time we may all be members of one body."

Maharshi Mahesh Yogi was among the first to suggest the *transcending process* characteristic of a field effect that brings about changes where distance is of no barrier—speculated that only a few people is what it takes to produce a global effect.

We learn in Applied Physics too that only a small quantity of particles has to change to effect a change of the whole. Magnetizing one percent of the atoms in a bar of iron results in the entire bar becoming magnetized. And chemical reactions also produce similar results; whereby as soon as a small portion of a solution is triggered, the remaining reaction takes place spontaneously.

Each of us is part and parcel of the whole. As a cell is to the body, the individual is to the cosmos. In the web of life, we are all tied together in this matrix. And in the superb words of Einstein: "each of us is an integral part of all life in this unending stream."

The boundaries dividing us are next to negligible. Somewhere in the equation is a Universal Mother/Father that encompasses our extended identities. And what else can this be other than the role we attribute to God—our Divine Parentage that makes our cosmic identity undeniably true!

In support thereof, Deepak Chopra recounted as follows:

"As is the human body, so is the cosmic body
As is the human mind, so is the cosmic mind.
As is the microcosm, so is the macrocosm.

* * *

The inner intelligence of the body is the ultimate
and supreme genius in nature.
It mirrors the wisdom of the cosmos.
This genius is inside you—
a part of your inner blue print
that cannot be erased.

* * *

The universe operates through dynamic exchange:
Giving and receiving are different aspects
of the flow of energy in the universe.
There's dynamic exchange of intelligence
between microcosm and macrocosm,
between human body and universal body,
between human mind and cosmic mind."

—Deepak Chopra

THE MACRO OR UNIVERSAL SOUL THEORY
THE UNDERLINING BRAHMAN

"I am the soul that dwells
in the heart of every mortal creature."

—Sri Krishna

Having put all the pieces of the puzzle together, we can now see the picture very clearly. Alone in the beginning, God became divisible like parts of the jigsaw puzzle we are trying to piece back here together. It was the creative energy of Brahman what gave rise to the cosmos.

The point I am endeavoring to make is that this interconnectedness and shared intelligence is nothing but Brahman—the common denominator that operates very much like the Invisible Field physicists find so absorbing and intriguing.

Brahman or the manifested power of God is what's behind everything. It is the one indestructible, enduring reality—the common thread that underlines all of creation. As a screen serves as the background for moving pictures in cinematography, so too Brahman is the substratum of the universe—the basis or foundation of everything.

Brahman is supremely above time, space and causation—traits not uncommon to the soul as well. As the individual soul is the unchanging reality behind the changing body, similarly the unchanging reality behind the changing universe is Brahman!

Making himself ostensibly clear, Sri Krishna trumpeted these glad tidings:

> *"Part of myself is the Brahman (God)*
> *found within every creature.*
> *And when Brahman is lodged within the individual*
> *it is called the Atman (soul).*
> *The creative energy of Brahman*
> *is what causes all existence to come into being.*
> *The power behind all is Brahman!"*
> *—The Gita*

"Part of myself is the polymorphous Brahman (God) within every creature." This communiqué categorically affirms the fact that the soul of man and God is in no way different. And in his own words, He further stated that: "When Brahman is lodged within the individual it is called the *Atman* (soul)."

The Over-soul or Universal Soul Theory purports that the soul is one and self-existent—that there is really speaking this oneness everywhere. He who comprehends this sees all beings in the Self, and the Self in all beings. All there is God, and, God is all there is—attesting to which here's what the Holy Upanishads promulgate:

"He who knows Brahman to be the eye of the eye,
the ear of the ear, the mind of the mind, the life of life,
he indeed comprehends fully the cause of all causes.
In Brahman there's no diversity.
He who sees diversity goes from death to death."

The end result is that like attracts like. Being part and parcel Brahman, the soul would ultimately revert or relapse back to Brahman—fuse and become one with it once again. From Brahman came man, and unto Brahman shall he return. We go back from whence we came!

It appears as if both religious and scientific evidences are pointing to the one and same conclusion: That there is this unifying, invisible field, holding all of nature together. And this Universality Theory would be further developed in the following chapter. But for now I shall end with this slight divulgence here.

EXTRAORDINARY PHENOMENA

When one considers such phenomenon as *synchronicity* (a term invented by social scientists to explain things that are not mere coincidences), one may conclude that perhaps there's an outside force greater than what our minds can possibly conceive—someone who organizes events in such a intricate manner as to determine otherwise inexplicable outcomes.

Take for example what is mentioned in Chopra's book. He gave us these examples to conder:

The infamous incident involving Titanic and the iceberg.

Identical twins.

Two persons born under the same planetary conditions tying the matrimonial knot.

Look-alike individuals having a common name.

Someone who at the very last minute decides against boarding an airplane that later on crashes.

Parents who could tell the exact moment their sons were killed in battle.

Call it whatever you like: clairvoyance, ESP, dreams, synchronicity. Aren't these all telling examples of glimpses into the mind of God—the signaling of a higher power above? Whether faintly or dramatically, God is sending us clues and warnings all the time. He is mailing us messages from outside time and space boundary—his outside world trying its level best to communicate with us!

And this reminds me of the story of my life. The day I got married, I presented Savitri with what I thought was a worthwhile gift: A plan of our life together. And speaking about mindset, in it I envisaged we would pursue our studies abroad and settle down there permanently—not discounting the fact that I shall retire early at age 40.

And so said, so done. I moved abroad, graduated and had my house all paid with enough money in the bank to retire at age 40. I became a millionaire. But instead of sticking to my guns, I fired off in a totally new direction. I decided to expand my Real Estate Business by purchasing a Franchise.

It turned out that on the very day I was to sign the dotted line, I got into a car accident on my way over to do so. And taking it to be a bad omen, I turned back and headed straight to my office. And relating to my secretary what had happened, these were my parting words to her: "I think God is stopping me doing this. I am not going ahead with the purchase."

But unstoppable and irrepressible as I was back then, two weeks later there was a complete change of heart. I went against my instincts and bought the darn thing! And right after executing the agreement, it was required of me to fly over with my wife to the states for a special orientation ceremony. And you wouldn't believe what had happened again!

The day we got there I was involved in another car-accident. This time I had with me my entire family. And to add insult to injury, it so happened that on the very same day also someone picked my pocket on the busy streets of New York City.

Sure, my heart missed a couple of beats! But I simply brushed it all aside thinking it to be superstitious and unmanly. I wrote them off as being isolated incidences—things that have absolutely no correlation or relevance to what I'm about to do. But how much more foolish and wrong can one be!

As ill luck would have it, this is how it all ironically paned out. Just a few months after I got started with my new company, the Real Estate market took a nosedive (it was during the recession of the late 1980s and early 1990s). And there I was left holding the bag after all my agents jumped ship—except three loyal, diehard men: Daywan, Kashmir and Sheer.

One thing led to another! And in the end, I found myself in a state of insolvency having to rebuild my life all over again from scratch. But thank God, I was able to rebuild my life quicker the second time around—not something I am teetering or reeling from today.

Strangely enough though, none of this would have happened if only I was paying heed. But just that I didn't know of this Great "Living" God before—someone like Him who would take an abiding interest over the diminutive and insignificant me.

An oxymoron may be, but it is personal tragedies such as these that eventually lead one unto God. I have chosen to include this incident of my life just in order to show you how connected our lives are with God—completely woven in the tapestry of existence overall.

And now I trust that you would appreciate why I sound so convinced and speak so much in the affirmative when it comes to God—touching off the most sensitive strands in my body.

❈ *Five* ❈

Where Science stops the Vedas begin

THE TRANSCENDENTAL STATE OF BEING

*"All living creatures at birth are led astray
by the delusion that this relative world is real."*
—*The Gita*

IN certain major areas of concerns science is still at its infantile or experimental stages of development, sadly lagging behind the Vedas. And as far as the methodical and untiring rishis were concerned, nothing is ever glyptically carved in stone—nay, not even what may be so inscribed by scientists even!

UNREALITY OF THE WORLD

One of the basic idiosyncrasies and belief of the rishis has to do with the unreality of the world—its fleeting and transitory nature. As perceived by our senses, the world looks, feels and appears real, which, from a cursory point of view, certainly looks that way. But three of the world's most renowned physicists (Einstein, Bohr and Heisenberg) saw that the accepted way of looking at the universe was false. What they discovered was that even though it does appear real, there is really no such proof.

Ontologically speaking, the rishis also saw no differently. They held out that the world is like a *dream*. By no means autistic in their upbringing, they viewed the treasures of the world as alluring mirages. Thrown at us just in order to test the true capacity of our resistance, it saw us failing to measure up to expectations.

The rishis declared that it is due to the illusive power of *maya* (a state of being whereby we see the things of the world as being real when in fact they are not)—an illusion brought upon us because of our imperfect, distorted human vision.

Having taken for granted that the world is real, we ought to be reminded that we are relying upon a wrong assumption. And fraught with error too, our actions undoubtedly leads us to bondage and suffering—having to free ourselves from which here's what Einstein in his profound wisdom had to say:

> *"The world is a kind of*
> *optical delusion of consciousness;*
> *and our task must be to*
> *free ourselves from this prison*
> *by widening our circle of compassion—*
> *embrace all living creatures and*
> *creation in its beauty."*

TIME AND SPACE

One of Einstein's most brilliant contributions to modern science has to do with his intuitive knowledge that *linear time* is superficial. He found that *time* can contract or expand depending on the *state of mind* of the observer.

Isn't it true that *time* literally flies when we are having fun or doing something pleasant? Take for instance talking to someone with whom we are in love. Wouldn't you say *time* quickly passes you by unnoticed? And don't we find *time* unduly prolonged when faced with an ominous or painful task? Take for example having to sit on needles edge. And in ratification thereto, another prominent physicist John Whealer made a rather strong and prophetic statement in this regards. He claimed that "the very idea of *space-time* is erroneous. And with that failing, the idea of before and after is also failing."

MATTER AND ENERGY

Even before the advent of the *theory of relativity*, considered one of the most profound acts of thought, *time, space, matter* and *energy* were thought to be unrelated and interchangeable. As a matter of fact, physicists had them placed in separate, watertight compartments.

It was not until Einstein published his most famous equation ($E=MC^2$) that the whole spectrum of things got radically changed. He had conclusively proven that *matter* could indeed be transformed into energy—a case in point being Atomic Bombs that are capable of producing an enormous amount of energy.

And Einstein's *Theory of Relativity* later did the same thing where *space* and *time* were concerned—resulting in scientists no longer treating them as being separate or independent of each other. In fact, they are now seen as a fused entity labeled *space-time*.

As it becomes more obvious that nature is less compartmentalized than was once thought, the *Theory of Relativity* opened up quite a few other doors for us—give rise to much more startling possibilities.

UNIFIED FIELD THEORY

Building on these hypotheses, Einstein further postulated that there has to be a common, underlying field serving as a background in the interchangeability between *space-time* and *matter-energy*—emphasizing the point that there exists a level in nature that is totally fused called *space-time-matter-energy*. And this is in no way different from what the like-minded rishis thought of Brahman as being the common denominator underlying all of creation.

As the name suggests, the *Unified Field Theory* effectively pulled together and provided a common basis for everything. It unites the basic forces in creation and explains why the cosmos is a composite whole—just as candidly declared by the much defiant and zealot rishis!

Following the same line of reasoning, Chopra is quoted as follows: "This *Unified Field* is inside all of us—anchoring us to the timeless world with every breath, every thought, every action. We are timeless essence, pure spirit, unbounded intelligence. Dynamic power is inherent in the *Unified Field,* Einstein and the ancient rishis shared in their vision.

The fact is that some people are more aware of this connection than others. And for those of us who do, death becomes less threatening."

HOW THE RISHIS SEE THE WORLD

The unwearied and tireless rishis too thought that nature was at some point unified. And to prove their ingenuity they came up with the missing link or part of the puzzle—one that would not fade away like the mist of illusion.

Being investigators into *transcendental reality,* they traveled on a road different to the one traversed by physicists—though very much in the same direction. In their inquisition they had to make a detour away from the accepted norms of science—resorted to a much more subjective rather than objective type of reasoning.

The reason why they went this route wasn't because they were incapable of conducting scientific experimentations. In fact, the Vedas are considered a compendium of science—including medicine, biology, botany, astrology and all other facets of human learning.

Brilliant empiricists as they were, the rishis found that certain phenomena in life do not readily lend themselves to scientific scrutiny. Take for example things that go beyond the realms of sensory perceptivity. Then looking for some form of rationality, the sagacious ones began looking first internally rather than externally.

Considered a contrariety or paradox of our time, it is regrettable that we have landed man on the moon but yet-for-all failed to conquer the world right within. And interestingly enough, therein lies the marvel of all marvels: Calmly sitting inside is the inner-man fully illumined as if by solar radiance, and, not just some mere lunar glow.

Here's how it is succinctly put in the Holy Upanishads:

"The Lord perceives the senses to turn outwardly.
Thus we look externally and see not the Self within.
A sage withdraws his senses from the outer-world
and seeks the hallowed state of immortlity—
looks within and beholds the deathless Self!"

Delving deep inside, they intuitively detected that reality begins with our conscious awareness. And after much probing thereto, they concluded that at any given point in time a person is said to be in one of three states of subjective awareness as follows:
1. Waking
2. Dreaming (sleeping)
3. Deep dreamless-sleep

TURIYA OR THE FOURTH STATE

Having thus subdivided and categorized man's state of awareness, the rishis then took a closer and more objective look. And having done so, they circumspectly detected that between each state lies a gap—one that acts very much like a pivot as we slide-pass one state into another.

In falling asleep, for example, the mind transcends the waking state by withdrawing the senses and shutting us out to the outside world. It is at this juncture, just before falling asleep, that a brief gap exists—likened unto a little window that can be classified neither as wake nor sleep. Because of this very faint and tiny gap there seems to exist a Fourth State—this intermediary or interstitial state that does not fit within the wake and/or sleep definition. And no matter how infinitesimally small it may seem, there remains a dividing line between those two states.

There's also a fleeting *gap of silence* between each thought harbored, wrote Dr. Chopra who also embraces the *Gap Theory*. And if it weren't for this, our thinking and manner of speech would have been just as confusing—a real mumble jumble. It would be like speaking in this gobbledygook manner: *TheRishisarevegetarians* (The rishis are vegetarians).

Try speaking like this and see what happens. So that what we say makes sense, there has to be a gap between each word uttered. And no matter how slick and unctuous it may be, the fact remains there has to be this gap.

PROOF OF THE FOURTH STATE

Many researches and scientific experiments are being conducted today to determine the beneficial effects of meditation. Dr. Robert Keith Wallace made one such notable attempt. In 1967 at UCLA, he had conclusively proven that Transcendental Meditation (TM) has some of the many benefits enumerated below.

He took several individuals practicing meditation and subjected them to various biomedical experimentations. And the data gathered, including the physiological changes the body undergoes, was monitored. But although he did not set out to prove the existence of the Fourth State, this was precisely what he did.

Here's some of the excellent benefits of TM:

1. Deep Relaxation: Meditators enter a state of deep relaxation never seen nor heard-of before.
2. Slower Breathing: TM results in a lower metabolic rate or level of energy consumption.
3. Reduced Oxygen Consumption: There is a reduction of almost 16%.
4. Decreased Heart Rate: Results in in-exhaustion to ones heart—herald a sense of great relief for heart patients.
5. Deep Rest: Found to be twice as deep-sleep the moment one closes his eyes.
6. Better Health: One enjoys a better state of mental and physical wellness.
7. Younger Looking: Compared to ones chronological age, the participants look and feel much younger.
8. Greater Clarity of Mind: There is this rejuvenation of mind, body and spirit—likened unto locating the roots of a plant and watering it.
9. Tranquility: Results in inward peace and bliss—a state of profound knowingness and vast expansion.
10. Spiritual Awaking: Reaching deep inside and changing the hidden blue print of intelligence, the individual is transported to a state of spiritual ecstasy.
11. Heightened awareness: While the body is completely relaxed as in deep-sleep, the mind remains fully alert—there is this prevailing sense of heightened awareness.

Chopra points out that 'the cerebral cortex of the brain automatically gets altered the moment one closes his eyes and relaxes. The dominance of alpha wave rhythms signals a state of rest and awareness all at the same time—sleeping and thinking being completely eliminated. Then corresponding changes occur in the body as blood pressure and heart rate decrease, accompanied by lessened oxygen consumption.'

CONCLUSIONS DRAWN

Wallace has proven that during meditation one is transported to a state that does not readily fit into any of the standard classifications mentioned herein before— namely, waking, dreaming or dreamless sleep.

For instance, it has been determined that one finds himself in a state twice as deep as deep-sleep while still maintaining heightened awareness. In other words, while enjoying optimum rest obtainable only during deep-sleep, one is still very much awake and alert.

TM gives rise to this intervening or intermediary state that characteristically does not fit within the wake, dream or dreamless-sleep categories. And going back to our previous discussions regarding the gap, we saw the same thing happening too just before falling asleep.

These findings verify delineation of the Fourth State of consciousness. And this validation by Wallace gave credence to what the Vedic masters were saying all along pertaining to the indefinable Fourth State or *turiya*. Then quite frankly, here's the proof we've been looking for!

Thus, he has given authenticity to both TM and *mind/ body connection* discussed in a previous chapter. And the conclusion drawn here is that, having reached this most exquisite state, it is like extending an invitation to a Higher reality, emphasized Dr. Chopra.

In furtherance thereof, the rishis discovered that when this state is reached the mind is emptied of all specific thoughts. And this being the case then, one is left with a clear and profound awareness that "I know everything."

He who discovers this state is beyond grief and despair—reaching which, sickness, old age and death are completely obliterated. Put differently, it is the state beyond subjective experience, beyond the senses, beyond understanding, beyond expression—a state of pure unitary consciousness.

And elucidating further, the rishis tabled this shocking revelation:

> *"The life of man is divided between*
> *waking, dreaming and dreamless sleep.*
> *But transcending these three states*
> *is super conscious vision—*
> *known as the fourth.*
> *The fourth, say the wise,*
> *is not subjective experience,*
> *nor objective experience,*
> *nor intermediary of the two,*
> *nor a negative condition.*
> *And neither is it also consciousness,*
> *nor unconsciousness.*
> *It is not the knowledge of the senses,*
> *nor is it relative knowledge,*
> *nor even inferential knowledge.*
> *Beyond the senses,*
> *beyond understanding,*
> *beyond expression is the fourth.*
> *It is pure unitary consciousness—*
> *wherein awareness of the world in all*
> *its multiplicity is completely obliterated.*

> *It is ineffable peace.*
> *It is the supreme good.*
> *It is the one without a second.*
> *It is the Self—know it alone!"*

THE NEED FOR MEDITATION

Having established the incalculable benefits derived from TM, let us for a moment or two put ourselves in the shoes of the learned rishis. They came to the realization that seeking the changeless (the Self) in the world of change (the body), they had to undertake the most daring journey through the regions of the mind and the world within.

And in so doing, they were able to discover the deathless Self that lies beyond sense perceptivity—reachable only by transcending all boundaries and going far beyond. And this subjective approach implemented by the rishis in anchoring oneself to the Self is known as *yoga*.

And being a form of *yoga*, meditation is that vehicle employed to fathom our human existence—an improvisation or means of locating the realm of quietude that is in each and every one of us. It brings about a state of awareness of *who* and *what* we are—the inner-man we seek and long to know.

As oceanographers devise ways-and-means to delve to the bottom of the ocean in an attempt to uncover hidden treasures, so too in nonetheless scientific manner the rishis were able to descend deep down into their super conscious zones and homes of beatitude.

It is a scientifically proven fact that the intensity of light increases as one gets closer to its source. And similarly so too the mind becomes more and more charged as it gets towards the Transcendental Field—charmed and evocatively drawn towards it.

It is the essential nature for man to be peaceful and

happy. And he who has lost these important ingredients in his life verily defeats the purpose of it. And realistically speaking, the main design or purpose of meditation is to locate that all important *soul-force-field*.

PRINCIPLES OF MEDITATION

Meditation is a household word toady. It began riding the crest of popularity somewhere between the sixties and seventies. Thanks to the efforts of Maharshi Mahesh Yogi who first introduced it to the Western World.

Meditation nevertheless took birth and was practiced as part of the great spiritual tradition of the Indian Vedic seers several thousands of years ago. Well-known for its stress, relaxation and therapeutic values in the West, it served a much higher purpose in the lives of its inventors.

Coined by Maharshi Mahesh Yogi, the word *transcendental* was later added in order to emphasize the importance for the mind to go beyond the shield of physical consciousness—to fathom that infinite, abstract field of supreme consciousness.

It is a natural tendency for us to go from the disturbed physical state to the more unruffled realm of the Self—to move to a field of greater happiness. And it should be mentioned that if left to its own freewill, the Self will naturally seek-out the peaceful domain of *turiya*.

Our normal level of consciousness occupies a small band at the surface; and only what's transpiring here we are aware of. But if broaden to span the entire depth, it would result in us becoming more or less super-conscious individuals. And wouldn't that be nice?

Our goal is to reach into the very depths—the seabed in the ocean of existence and awareness. And only by achieving this would we be able to gain empowerment in the entire level of subtlety—the powerhouse and home of out true transcendental Selves.

CENTRAL THEME

The central theme of meditation is that we become what we meditate on. And needless to say, our goal is to meditate and establish an intimate relationship with our souls—that inherent Brahman or God in us. And by aligning ourselves to such authentic empowerment, we become nearly as powerful as God Himself.

And while we are on this topic, how about I share with you a thought that readily comes to mind. It has been shown that every thought, word and action of ours produces an influence on our environment in a positive or negative way.

Therefore, you would want to think its a good idea to selectively produce good vibrations only—ones that would give rise to feelings of happiness and harmony. And blessed as we are, man possesses a highly developed and much evolved nervous system to do precisely just that— to voluntarily produce thoughts of a purer and subtler nature.

THE PRIMORDIAL SOUND OM

"When Om unceasingly reverberates
within the heart of an aspirant
he feels deeply loved and blessed."

—Yama

Quickly reviewing what was said before, we saw that in the beginning the *word* was with God. And synonymous to God, that *word* was in fact *Om*. And in it was found compressed divine intelligence.

"And without it was anything made that was made"— the Biblical connotation here being that this mother sound somehow broke the cosmic silence and gave birth to the universe. It somehow got transformed into an enormous amount of matter and energy in form of creation.

And evidently so, even Brahman is referred to as *Om,* which, when it reverberates in the heart if an aspirant, brings about a remarkable sensation to the spirit of man. And it is believed that by simply repeating this word, the secrets of the Mother of the Universe shall unlock themselves unto us.

Although there are many forms of meditation, the most advanced type has the word *Om* included right into the *mantras* (secret formulas) used in conjunction thereto. And without question, *Om* is the most essential part in these *mantras*—invariably the first word in all such mystic syllables prescribed by a qualified guru.

Incorporating *Om* in all its primordial power serves as a reminder as to what station in life we ought to be tuned in to. This is a very important consideration—and one too that should not be taken too lightly. Unparalleled and immeasurable as the benefits are, we must make it a habit repeating *Om* until it has attained some form of consistency in us.

This is how Chopra saw it: "Some orthodox Hindus would say that every *mantra* is a different version of God's name, while others would claim and this is very close to quantum physics that the vibration of the *mantra* is the key here. The word *vibration* means the frequency of brain activity in the cerebral cortex. The *mantra* forms a feedback loop as the brain produces the sound, listens to it, and then responds with a deeper level of attention. Mysticism isn't involved."

And later on we shall see how beneficial the repetition of *Om* is to a dying person. Coupled with meditation, it would pilot the mind towards the Virtual Domain of God— enable him to achieve oneness with God in the end.

✣ *Six* ✣

The Law of Karma and Reincarnation

*"Karma is the general assertion
of human freedom.
Our thoughts, words, deeds
are threads of the net
we throw around ourselves."*
—Swami Vivekananda

USED in everyday conversation today, *karma* is a word we are all quite familiar with. And the concept derives repute from of its uniqueness—there being no other theory that comes close enough in explaining the criterion of *Reincarnation* and *Life after Death*.

Karma is defined as ones volitional acts that determine his place in the Cycle or Wheel of Birth and Death prior to obtaining a final release from this world. It's the sum total of all actions accomplished in one stage of a person's life that determines his destiny in the next.

After such an intellectual and scholarly definition, I shall now break it down in bits and pieces for you. And in so doing I propose to take you through the peaks and valleys of it all—explore the full karmic implications of our multifaceted thoughts, words, deeds, feelings, emotions.

THE LAW OF CAUSATION

The Law of Causation governs our actions both in the

physical and psychological planes. There is no effect without cause—or cause without effect. Nothing one says, thinks, does is without its dire consequences and repercussions—no escaping the aftermath and ripple effects of our reprehensible wrongdoings.

It has been scientifically determined that every action generates a force of energy that rebounds in equal proportions. Just as there can be no basic loss of *matter* nor *energy,* similarly there can be no action without a corresponding reaction—a reciprocal counteraction that is.

And this brings us to Newton Law of Motion, which incontestably states that: *To every action there is an equal and opposite reaction*—a direct inference to the Law of Karma if I may say so.

Not only externally, but, internally too, the Law of Karma is operative. And a good example is how our thoughts affect the physiological functioning of our bodies: Whereas a destructive reaction such as *anger* releases toxin that lowers our resistance, a positive one such as *patience* protects and heals—meaning that we are punished for being angry and rewarded when patient.

Thus I am a very careful person where casting aspersions are concerned—the making of condescending and disparaging remarks. He who thinks he can hurt another person (or creature) without himself first getting hurt is sadly mistaken indeed. Somewhere, somehow, it will all come back to haunt you. What goes around, comes around—as you make your bed so muse you lie in it.

If, for instance, you seek a loving and compassionate world, all that is required of you is to be loving and compassionate yourself. And since *like attracts like,* it would attract other souls of like frequency unto you— attribute to a much more loving and compassionate world. It all revolves around what you do.

Karma works in such a trenchant manner that even

ones dreams or wishes can have a piquant effect. If, for example, one wills a harmonious spousal relationship more than an inharmonious one, the dynamics would fall in favor of ones marriage saved as opposed to being ruined—wound up in a divorce.

The Theory of Karma also recognizes the paramount Rule of Law, whereby justice is always served. One does not have the liberty to take the law into his own hands. And neither is there the need for an Appellate Court (Appeal Court) since miscarriage of justice is never an issue—the brandishing of the Mighty Sword of Justice in the name of *karma*.

An aphorism I particularly like and find rather neat is: *You break the law, you pay the price.* If we perform actions that are incompatible to Nature and God, there needs be no Celestial Law Giver to strike us down. Believe it or not, we are cursing our own selves when we do.

This is suggestive of the fact then that one should never be on the wrong side of the law. Do not contravene it by any means. We all do have the tendency to want to bend it at times, but break it we must not. And if we do, we would see for ourselves the writings on the wall.

GENERAL APPLICABILITY

"The wages of sin is death!"
—*The Holy Bible*

Nothing in this world goes unpaid—is left up to chance. There is no guessing, no hit and miss, no ifs and buts. The oracular Law of Karma works in such a way that the discriminating man is held fully accountable for his actions—answerable to God at all times.

No one, small or great, is above the long arm of the Law of Karma. And there are absolutely no strings to pull, or favors granted either. Irrespective of whom or what you are, this most irrefragable and incontrovertible law exacts its pound of flesh. Each of us must fetch the burden of our own sins and retributions.

Everything in this universe is precisely and meticulously regulated. It's the governing principle orchestrated by the wisest of them all. And barring divine interventions, there's no exceptions, impartiality, favoritism, corruption—nor do recognizances are of any avail too.

God does not unnecessarily wants to punish his children. No good father would! And blasphemous as it is even to suggest such a thing, it wouldn't be the God whom we would want to worship either—sounds more like a sadistic monster to be avoided and abhorred.

What God really wants is for us to be good children—obedient to his laws. And as such you would find the declaration of the Holy Upanishads quite relevant to our discussions here:

> *"As a man acts, so shall he become.*
> *A man of good deeds becomes good.*
> *A man of evil deeds becomes evil!"*

NEGATIVE KARMA

> *"Judge not that ye be not judged.*
> *For with what judgment ye judge*
> *ye shall be judged.*
> *With what measure ye mete*
> *it shall be measured unto thee."*
>
> —The Blessed Lord Jesus

Speaking about value judgment, the Golden Rule states it best: *Do unto others as you would have them do unto you*—implying that when we harm others we create negative *karma*.

And don't be fooled either if the penalty is not immediately meted out unto you, for there is usually this

holdover clause that states: *An action not brought to fruition is one that has not yet taken effect—met its end.*

In God's Plan or Scheme of Things, no moratorium is
ever granted. It's a doctrine that dictates a perfect cosmic
balance of energy. Any seeming imbalance is simply in the
process of sorting itself out. And this, cautioned the rishis,
do not necessarily have to be in this lifetime either.

The *Bible* states it well: "Cast thy bread upon the waters
and it shall come back to you after many years." Everything
has a way to balance itself out in the end no matter how
long it takes. It will sooner or later take its toll. These are
the dictates of the infallible and irrefutable Law of Karma.

RECIPROCITY

The farthest thing from the truth is the notion often expressed: *You can't take it with you.* I agree, name, fame,
money, you can't—reason being they are so transient and
diurnal in nature. They could, without notice, be easily
swept away at any given moment.

But as night follows day, a man takes along with him
his *karma*—gets what's coming to him. In fact, he can't even
leave them behind even if he wants to. As your shadow
follows you, so does too your *karma,* good or bad. Its
something you just cannot extricate yourself from no matter how hard you may try to.

Every man gets his dues. As one fashions his tools and
dwelling, so does too his destiny. We are of our own making. Whatever we are today is as a result of what our
thoughts and actions were yesterday. A man reaps whatever he sows—gets out of life precisely what he puts into
it.

Fully commensurate on what we have expended and
given to the world, we become the prime recipient or ben-
eficiary thereof—nothing more, nothing less. You have

heard the saying before: *Man is an architect of his own destiny.* As the karmic pendulum swings, its outcome can in no way be sidestepped nor sidetracked.

Comes Doomsday (the Day of Judgment) we shall all be outmaneuvered—have our heads rolled if we are not careful. And in this Supernal Jurisdiction where God alone presides, our cause shall be contested purely on our karmic deeds.

And since the Day of Reckoning is neigh, one should live his life like an open book—be ready for inspection at all given times. Man may deceive his fellowman, but God he cannot. And even among men, we may fool some of them some of the time, but not all of them all the time.

DIVINE LAWS CANNOT BE AVOIDED

And moving right along, here's a real concern I've always had—and still do. Relying on the assumption that God is just and fair, then why is there so much of inequalities and disparities in life? Why are some born rich and others poor; some healthy and others unhealthy; some live a whole century while others die at birth if not before? Why?

We observe too that many possess great aptitude— excel at certain disciplines or sports. And they may even do so without any conscious efforts on their part! While there others, who, even with the greatest of exertions, are pail in comparison. Where is the justice here in all of this?

And if one tries to explain it using genetic models and other rationales, it may very well tell us *how* but certainly not *why*. You mean the human destiny is just a matter of luck and chance—determined just like the draw in a lottery? And if not accidental, why are there so much of incongruities and discrepancies in life then?

And claiming that we have just this one life to live further complicates matter—accounts for nothing being satisfactorily explained. Only the incontrovertible and unassailable Law of Karma can explain it all and still make perfect sense. And here's how the visionary rishis saw it all.

They most judiciously concluded that it is all due to the revival of past impressions—foregone deeds and actions. We carry with us the whole of our inerasable past—an ineffaceable record time cannot blur or death expunge.

Please remember always! There is absolutely no inheritance to count on—only the legacy we brought with us from preceding lives. And we are to add to this by leading a good and incorruptible life—take to the path of godliness.

A SPIRITUAL NECESSITY

Being God's Law, *karma* is not just a mere mechanical principle. And sin or negative *karma* is not so much a defiance of God as a disavowal and rejection of the soul—not so much a violation of the law as a betrayal and denial of the Self.

Considered one of India's modern day saints, Swami Vivekananda delivered this most impassioned and fervid speech at the First World Parliament of Religion in Chicago. Rising to a thunderous and deafening applause, he mesmerized the audience by his wonderful intonation—not to mention his profound wisdom.

As an ascetic, he evocatively displayed that conspicuous aura he had about him—one accentuated too by the way he attired himself. Simplistically dressed in his long flowing saffron robe, he griped the attention of all by this keynote speech of his—a portion of which is being reproduced here:

"Is man a tiny boat in a tempest
raised one moment on the foamy crest of a billow

and dashed down the next into a yawning chasm,
rolling to and fro at the mercy of good and bad actions—
a powerless, helpless wreck, in an ever raging,
uncompromising Current of Cause and effect.
Is he a little moth under the Wheel of Causation,
rolling and crushing everything in its way—
mindful not of the widow's tears nor orphan's cry?
The heart sinks at the idea,
yet this is the Law of Nature.
Is there no hope?
Is there no escape
was the cry that sprung from
the bottom of the heart of despair.
And reaching the Throne of Mercy
an inspired Vedic sage stood up and
offered the words of hope and consolation—
proclaimed in trumpet voice these glad tidings:
Hear ye children of immortal bliss,
even ye that resides in the higher spheres!
I have found that Ancient One
who is beyond all darkness and delusion.
Knowing him alone you shall be saved
over-and-over again from death!"

REINCARNATION

It is almost impossible to have a discussion on *karma* without looking at the corresponding principles of *Reincarnation and Transmigration of the Soul* running side-by-side—precepts the rishis themselves found quite fascinating and astounding.

When adjudged overall, there are compelling reasons to believe that we must have had a previous life—an insidious past we are all privy to. Do you ever notice when a newborn looks you in the eyes you want to believe for the life of you that an old soul is staring at you once again?

Reincarnation finds its general acceptability in that there is no other theory that can adequately explain why things are the way they are. Why, even though under the Guardian or Trusteeship of God, there is so much of inequalities, unfairness and injustices in the world.

What makes the concept even more credible is the fact that no one can refute it. Not even from the scientific camp is there forthcoming any confutation and rebuttal thereto—the world finding it increasingly difficult to discount any of it.

And in introducing the topic, I should mention that reincarnation is also a *doctrine of great hope*. Quixotic may be, but the fact remains that it is certainly a meaningful approach to life—a point of view best summed up in the words of that Great Soul Swami Pranavanandaji Maharaj: "Contraction is death—expansion life."

Just by merely believing in the hereafter sets the mind at ease—makes you want to jump for joy. And this in turn leads to a whole new exuberant you—makes your life more hopeful and/or purposeful.

Now with this exordium, let's now look at few of the many impregnable arguments there are in support of the Theory of Reincarnation. And they are outlined here for our full appraisal and due consideration.

FEAR OF DEATH

One may ask why this morbid, pathological and dreadful fear of death—this most horrific and infectious fear of all! There has to be an arguably good reason for this. And if I am to speculate, it seems as if we must have had some prior bitter experience—an impingement that leaves us in this very devastating and deleterious state of mind.

According to the Theory of Reincarnation, this experience is encoded a million times over in our subconscious minds. Therefore, its no wonder that man is so much pre-occupied over death—conscious of the gruesome fate awaiting him down the road.

This reminds me of an experience I've recently had with my grandson whose name is also Rishi. He wanted to know why we were not putting up the Christmas tree the year my mother died. And I had to explain to him that on ac-count of the death of his great grandmother, we were not going to celebrate Christmas that year— being a period of mourning as per tradition.

Having explained myself to him, he most wittingly in-terjected: "Nana (for grandfather) would I die also?" Taken aback at the nature of his inquiry, I was first tempted to cajole him into believing otherwise. But instead, I elected to test the capacity of his infantile mind to see what might be so registered.

And so I answered his question with a question: "What do you think Rishi?" And here the conversation took an even more bizarre twist—astounded and flabbergasted as his answer came back to hit me: "Yes nana, I have to die also, but I don't want to."

Incredible as it may sound, where on earth would a four year old, just weaned, got this from! And not because he is my grandson that I am using the term *child prodigy,* but in fact such precocious mental development is nothing but testamentary evidences of ones inextricable pass—a spillover from our previous lives.

LOVE AT FIRST SIGHT

Love *prima facie* (love at first sight) is yet another good ex-ample of there being a precursory relationship we might have had—a life antecedent to the one we are now enjoy-ing. Take your spouse for example! Meeting for the first time as perfect strangers, you then and there realized she's the one with whom you are going to tie the knot.

And while you were having these vibes, there she was entertaining the very same idea—the fact that the two of you might be just right for each other. Having once loved each other, those deeply imbedded or innate feelings were surfacing here once again. And being not an uncommon expression, wouldn't you say it holds particularly true here in your case: "I never felt like this before meeting someone for the first time."

Much to her shock and dismay, we learnt that Lord Buddha related to his wife her kindness towards him in a preceding life they were together—identifying others too who were in their lives. And so did too Lord Sri Krishna when he apprised Arjuna: "You and I have lived many times in the past; and while I remember them all, you don't."

BIBLICAL POINT OF VIEW

Not only Buddha and Sri Krishna gave the stamp of approval to the Theory of Reincarnation, but so too did Jesus indirectly. In all fairness though, he might not have uttered the word, though the question was put to him on more than one occasion. And the fact remains too that nowhere it is recorded that he ever condemned the doctrine—evoked in him a negative response.

As indicated by Jesus himself, Elijah was reborn as John the Baptist. And when the question was put to him by his disciple as to "which did sin, this man or his parents that he was born blind," Jesus replied "that the man's sins nor his parents' sin was the cause of his blindness—but that the work of God should be made manifest in him."

For all you know, Jesus did not rule out any preexistence of that man. Since neither that man's nor his parents' sin was the cause of his blindness, then it must have been

as a result of a sin previously committed—a direct inference to the Theory of Karma and Reincarnation he seemingly condoned.

COUNTER-ARGUMENT

Perhaps the only counter-argument that can be leveled
against reincarnation has to do with the fact that if there
is indeed life after death then why do we not remember
our past lives—made cognizant of our forgone existences?

As purported by the philosophy of *positivism,* only a fac-
tual encounter could conclusively settle the dispute—the
issue of whether or not there is life after death. And there
being no easy way out, speculation runs rampantly wild
in the minds of us all.

But the fact that we do not remember does not necessarily mean we haven't lived before. And I am very much
confident that the answer you are about to hear shall forever dispel this lingering doubt in your mind. And freed
from this paranoia, man shall hopefully lead a life of great
strides.

It can be argued that man's memory is shallow to begin
with. Could you precisely remember all what happened
yesterday—or for that matter an hour or so ago? And if you
are like me, I am sure you would have to admit your short-
comings when it comes down to remembering things.

Amounting to no more than a *partial memory,* man cannot remember everything that literally transpired in his life.
And even if he were to, certainly he cannot recount them
in the same sequence or chronological order it all happened.

The same can be said too about dreams—something we
are also prone to forget. And do we not also suffer long
lapses of consciousness when we are asleep? Summing up
it all, our memory is sketchy and faulty at best—which in

some ways too account for most of our childhood memories escaping us.

Being unable to remember one's childhood does not erase it by any means—which should also hold true for reincarnation. Seeing that our childhood is an experience we've most certainly had, how ludicrous would it be if we were to simply dismiss the idea! Just because we cannot remember something does not alter the reality of the situation.

And this brings us to the single most important reason why we cannot remember our past lives. Consumed by fire or decayed upon burial, the physical body suffers total annihilation after death—including the brain that houses the Faculty of Memory. And with the destruction of the entire Central Nervous System including the brain, how would it be possible for us to remember anything. And that's the end of the argument—period.

Like many psychologists, I am also of the opinion that it's perhaps better that way anyway—the fact that we do not remember our former lives. For one thing, it does not cheat or rob us the thrill of a lifetime. And in this way too, it even imparts more meaning to life—keeps it more suspenseful.

And nether is there this overcast of inhibition to deal with—being that man is reborn as a result of him failing to reach his ultimate goal. There is none of these feelings of guilt and inadequacy to deal with. And being a fact of life, it could have reduced ours to an awful state of drudgery and redundancy.

God in his infinite wisdom saw and intended differently. Studies have shown that people who seem to remember their past are constantly being haunted by their memories: Only gruesome incidences such as illness, crimes and murders standout—never seems the pleasant happenings!

OTHER STRONG EVIDENCES

The vast majority of us do harbor an inbred belief and conviction in the hereafter. Almost two-thirds of all Americans do. And history is also replete with testimonials of gifted people who maintain that they actually remember their previous lives—which I am sure is more of an anomaly rather than the general rule.

And in furtherance of the *theory of spiritualism and necromancy,* it is believed that the spirit of the dead communicates with the living. And there's an enormity of examples where deceased relatives, especially whom they were close to, visiting them just prior to death.

I personally know of individuals, who, moments before their death, saw and spoke of deceased loved ones—including my mother, who, on her deathbed, exclaimed to my sister present: "There goes my mother. There she is! Can't you see her?"

And while she was uttering these words, there stood my poor sister—utterly dumbfounded, stupefied and transfixed! Caught off-guard, she was unexpectedly rebuked by my mother for her unresponsiveness and seeming lack of interest.

But even more gripping is the claim coming from almost eight million Americans alone, who insist that they know what death is like. Having had a brush with it, many lived through such ordeals to give their vivid testimonies. And the list includes: Heart attacked victims, patients under the influence of anesthesia, and those who were already clinically pronounced dead!

It has been reported that these "death smitten" ones somehow miraculously survived and told of their amazing tales. They spoke of their out-of-body experiences—all curiously reporting a similar *transitional state* of leaving this world and going to another quite beyond.

Analyzing NDE's (the acronym for near death experiences), Moody in his book *Life after Life* looked at the other world journeys encountered by people who were on the brink of loosing their lives—all of whom strangely reported miraculous glimpses of the world yet to come.

They envisioned being in a state of peaceful existence and heavenly bliss. And appearing before them was this *light* reachable only by going through a small tunnel or passageway. In short, these people returned convinced that they have been to the Abode of God and were even bathed in the Divine Light.

Recapturing their mood, Moody in his other book *The Light Beyond* wrote: "NDE's experience all of the following events: A sense of being dead, peace and painlessness even during a seemingly painful experience, bodily separation, entering a dark region or tunnel, rising rapidly into the heaven, meeting deceased relatives and friends who are bathed in the light, encountering a Supreme Being, reviving one's life, feeling of reluctance to return to the world of the living."

And this reminds me of similar testimonies given by my late father Sriman Bechu Sangram Singh and teacher Babu Seeraj Singh—both of whom were quite religious-minded. At the point of their death, they found that the bedside wailing of loved ones completely distracted them—caused them to come back down to earth.

They saw these angel-like ones chanting the holy name of God. Drawn and captivated by what was going on, they were dying to join in the chanting themselves. But on account of the disturbance, they were prevented from so doing—for which they became very troubled at heart.

ENCOUNTERING GOD

It is not just a mere coincidence that NDE's are filled with references to light. Light fascinates us not only because it is one of the most perceptible forms of energy, but mainly because all the great religions of the world glorify and worship it. As a matter of fact, Hindu deities are depicted with a sort of incandescent and refulgent *auric field* (halo). And didn't the Lord Jesus too saw himself in the same light when he uttered the famous line of his: "I am the light of the world!"

What else can light be but *God-Force-Field.* In fact, God unquestionably enters the world as such. And even our most believable modern religion (science) traced light back to the very beginning of times—right back to creation itself.

As we get towards the end of the book, we shall learn how these rather lifting feelings and encounters with light are similar to what were experienced by the yogis when death was imminent. And when questioned further, they described this ultimate state of being by the choicest of words: *Enlightenment* and/or *illumination,* both strangely having to do with light!

MY PERSONAL EXPERIENCES

I now crave your indulgence as I sporadically interject anecdotes of my own life. And I trust that they would shed light to our discussion on near-death-experiences—regarded by many as being the *staircase to heaven.*

It so happened, as if by divine intervention, that something quite alarming happened to me in the midst of writing this book. For the very first time in my life I got really sick and had a close call with death. Taken ill all of a sudden, I had to undergo a quintuple opened heart bypass surgery.

And recovering in the Cardiac Intensive Care Unit immediately after surgery, I was told that when the nurse asked how I was feeling, my reply was: "I feel like being in heaven, and you look like a goddess"—words that presumably left the nurse feeling quite amused and flattered.

But like many who had undergone cardiac surgery and was under the influence of anesthesia, it is not uncommon to have near-death-experiences. And joggling my memory, I did recollect having expressed those sentiments—enveloped as I was in this exhilarating mood.

I saw this angel-like individual sitting on a high pedestal besides a pole light emitting the most beautiful glow— a sedative light overflowing with such quiescence. Overtaken by this enraptured and sensational feeling, I wholeheartedly wished it never did come to an end!

Having surrendered and resigned my life to God, I never attributed anything negative to my illness—nor to my life in general. I reasoned that if it's God's will, then so be it. God knows best what's night for me more than anyone else.

Everything that happens to us has a meaning and spiritual significance attached to it—a purpose and lesson to be learnt from it. There is a bright side to every mishap— a silver lining behind every dark cloud. It's a universe where God and not man is in control.

Therefore I thought to myself that perhaps God wanted me to have this firsthand near-death-experience—afford me the opportunity to have this empyrean glimpse of the world to come. That awaiting us in the yonder world is a life more rewarding and enchanting—this Elysium of unrestricted happiness men only dream of.

I'm convinced that in order to build us God first has to break us. Invasively or otherwise, he has to do what's deemed necessary—even if needs be to open our hearts and minds. And what I have been through made me appreciate life that much more. It made me a much stronger, God-fearing person—twice the man I was.

And despite what my allotment in life is, I have always drawn inspiration and live by the oracular injunctions of the scriptures—death-defying words such as the ones mentioned below meant to see us through the hurdles and misadventures of life:

> *"Yea though I walk through*
> *the valley of the shadow of death*
> *I will fear no evil*
> *for thou art with me—*
> *thy rod and staff comfort me!"*
>
> —*The Holy Bible*

PREMONITION OF DEATH

Worth exploring here is yet another alarming experience I've simultaneously had—another sudden twist of fate and defining moments of my life. It so happened that while I was hospitalized, my mother too became ill. And in retrospect now I want to believe that on account of her love for me she possibly gave up her life in order to save mine!

Actually, she went so far as to confide in one of my sisters that "I just cannot live to see another child of mine die before my eyes." Unfortunately, four had already gone to the Great Beyond—a state of doldrums she never quite got herself out of until her dying day.

Unlike her real self, she made it just once to see me in the hospital—the day after my surgery. And right after I came home, she badly wanted to pay me a visit, but, for one reason or another, it was met with undue delay. Three to four weeks went by like this. And by now you could imagine, the urge in her grew even more.

The day before her visit, she made plans with three of my sisters, uncle and aunt to accompany her. And after one of them wanted to postpone the visit for the following day, she expressed a grave sense of urgency: "I don't want another day to pass without having to see my son."

Little did they know that she was on a mission; and her real problem was that *time* was practically running out on her. And in hindsight now, I want to believe that she knew exactly what was ahead of her—conducting herself as someone who had come to give her blessings and bade us farewell.

What would turn out to be her last supper, it was a truly remarkable one. As we sat around the table, my uncle purposely brought and sat her next to me. And in many respect too, it bore the reminiscences of Jesus last supper with his disciples.

Having comfortably seated his disciples, Jesus ceased the opportunity to apprise them of his impending death. But the important difference here is that instead of having to reproach any of us, my mother was here to shower us with her parting love and benedictions.

Getting ready to leave our home that evening, she said goodbye and walked to the front door. And as she was about to go through, she requested of my wife to meet with me just once more—a request my wife most obligingly carried out.

And in a way she had never done before, she lavished me with such tender motherly love and affection—turning next to my wife and repeating herself. And thus she left, and it was for good. Next morning after her daily ablutions and prayers, she suffered myocardial infarction (massive cardiac arrest) that sent her straight into a coma—never again having to utter a single word to anyone.

Presumably having had premonition of her death, three weeks later she departed to the heavenly abode. And reviewing the sequence of events leading up to her demise, how much more certain can one be about presentiments— the foreboding and portentous presage of death.

SPEAKING ABOUT DREAMS

Dreams have been described as the *voice of nature* within us. Researches today have shown that dreams regulate and balance our physical and mental energies with our state of being. And typically among older people, it perforce psychically prepares them for the final episode.

Perhaps God has a real concern in wanting to pave the way for the ultimate destination awaiting us all. And it is not strange that right before my mother's death, she also spoke of the many dreams she was having—typically ones surrounding her deceased loved ones.

And as we are on the topic of dreams, how about I share with you a dream I once had. I dreamt that I died. And while my loved ones were grieving over my body, there I was, mounted on a high pedestal, silently witnessing what was happening. And not withstanding the lamentations all, I was totally unmoved—ever so much self-composed and unaffected.

Almost similar to the experience I've had during my surgery, it was a feeling beyond my wildest imagination. There was this inexplicable peacefulness and bliss overshadowing my entire being. Billed the *re-entry syndrome* by psychologists, I was reluctant to return to my former grievous sate of relative existence here on earth.

CONCLUSIONS

It is gratifying knowing that all of these evidences are pointing to one and same direction: That awaiting us down this thoroughfare is a guiding light and bright prospect of hope—perchance our only opportunity to meet vis-à-vis (face-to-face) with God. And that when this door closes, another will be opened unto us filled with blessedness. Incidences like these left me feeling personally convinced that there has to be some unknown mystery surrounding death—a plan God has kept concealed from us for one reason or another. And dying to know the truth myself, here I am conducting this thorough investigation resulting in the birth of this book.

And in the final analyses, I have to consider myself rather fortunate to be in this position. Thought to many it may appear as a somewhat unfortunate set of circumstances, to me it was just the opposite. Perhaps weak of flesh, but God wanted me to grow stronger in spirit—become unshakeable in my resolve.

As such I find the experience writing this book much to my satisfaction. And now beyond the measure of all doubts, I stand before the world most convinced and full of optimism where the ultimate fate awaiting us is concerned—described by some as being the *Journey into the Unknown*.

❋ *Part Three* ❋

JOURNEY INTO THE UNKNOWN

Objectives

Dialogue with Death
Here's an effective way to set the stage for any ensuing discussions on death—a tale in form of a very stimulating dialogue.

The Building Blocks
And after this all-embracing dialogue, we shall elaborate further on the more important themes introduced here—highlight those concept considered vital to our understanding of death.

✳ *Seven* ✳

Dialogue with Death

I N the introduction of this rather invigorating dialogue with death taken from the *Katha Upanishad*, I want to draw this parallel between the episodes in the lives of Buddha and Nachiketa—one of the two principal characters named herein.

A GLIMPSE OF BUDDHA'S LIFE

The pains and sufferings of the world cut deep into the heart and soul of the sympathetic and ruthful Buddha— added poignancy to his conviction of the unreality of all things finite. And as destiny would have it, it was prognosticated that there will come a day when he would forsake his royal dispositions all in search of the Eternal Truth.

And due to this prophecy, his father kept him quarantined within the confines and precincts of the palace— never allowed him the opportunity to see the outside world. But when he was sixteen, he requested that he be allowed to see the rest of the kingdom—a request his father granted only after much deliberations.

On the day he was given permission to go, it was ordered that the sick and seniors be kept away from the streets. But in spite of these precautions, Buddha nevertheless spotted this deformed, emaciated old man—a plight he never encountered before.

"What has become of this man?," he inquired in pity from his charioteer Channa. And unhesitatingly Channa answered: "He has been overtaken by old age—a fate that awaits us all." "Even my wife and new born son," interjected Buddha! "All," came the reply.

The next day he ventured out again. This time he noticed someone who was quite ill and in deep agonizing pain. "Does this too happen to all?," questioned Buddha. "To all. As the body grows old it cannot escape deterioration and degeneracy," Channa pointed out.

Yet the following day he went out again. And for the very first time in his life he was confronted with the death of someone—there was this funeral procession passing. And even before he could get a word in, Channa graciously volunteered: "Yes sire, this too happens to all. As the body ages, death has to come."

Buddha was shattered to pieces upon hearing this. Such travesty, burlesque and caricature nature characterizing all of life, he wondered. Yet-for-all, as he looked around he saw how inconsiderate it was of his subjects to be engaging themselves in the nugatory and trumpery aspects of life (pleasure-seeking)—knowing fully well that what await them down the corridor is sickness, old age and death!

But it so happened that on the fourth day he was greeted with something quite extraordinary. He saw this man contemplatively seated, absorbed in meditation. "He is seeking the Eternal—that which they say is beyond all changes and sorrow," explained the informed Channa.

And that was the turning point in the life of the postulant Buddha! Prompted and driven as if by a deep sense of urgency, he then and there instantaneously made up his mind to forsake everything in search of *nirvana*—a challenge the enlightened one met with resounding success.

NACHIKETA

As the mythological story has it, there came a day when Nachiketa's enraged father castigated him—ruthlessly decided to hand him over to Yama the king of death. Smitten with fear, the lad immediately began contemplating on death—conducting himself with such urgency as if he was about to be snatched away that very moment.

As if a trapdoor suddenly opened up in his mind, he began pondering what it would be like to taste of death. "Death has undone so many before—man, woman and children alike. Not millions, but billions have already gone before. But whereto," he wondered.

With such troubled mind Nachiketa wanted answers. And not any roundabout and evasive ones would suffice either. Out of the horse's mouth must he hear for himself what lies beyond death's door—a confession mankind has not been fortunate enough to elicit from Yama.

THE BACKGROUND

Thousand of years ago, there was this saga involving a youngster by the name of Nachiketa. His father, a charismatic expotus and mogul by today's standard, possessed great status whereby the entire community looked up to him in deep respect and admiration. And like many in his position would do in those days wanting to flaunt his wealth, he ostentatiously announced plans of making a munificent donation (gift) done by way of performance of some ancient rites and rituals.

He stipulated and made it abundantly clear that he was

going to give away all his possessions. And included were his cows, considered at the time the legal tender. But behind it all he was full of ulterior motives—had premeditated ideas of his own, which was ostensibly made clear to his son alone.

What Nachiketa observed his conceited and uncouth father doing was selectively going through his possessions, and, in a mean spirited and parsimonious manner, getting rid only of the worthless ones—surreptitiously and stealthily parting with cows on their last lap, feeble and old.

Wondering what religious merit might accrue to one making such worthless gifts, Nachiketa in protest thereto discreetly stuttered words of objection into the ears of his belligerent and obdurate father. But amenable not to his request, he nonetheless pretentiously went ahead with his plans—going about same in the most causal and nonchalant manner.

Seeing that he was one of his possessions too, he wanted to know of his father why he was not parting with him also. Provokingly he asked not once, not twice, but thrice. And infuriated as his father became, he, with a grimacing look in the face, impetuously blurted out in insurgence thereto: "I'll give you to death."

Such pungent and acrid words, wondered Nachiketa as the wrath of his disgruntled and chagrined father fell upon him. Inadvertently perhaps meant he those words— the sounds of which echoed and re-echoed in the ears of the much distraught, perplexed young man.

"How officious coming from ones own biological father," marveled Nachiketa. But as a subterfuge or stratagem to save face, he, in the exigency of the situation, had to quickly come up with a way to shut him up less his actions be seen hypocritical—his reputation got ruined.

Seeking not to vilify nor condemn his father, Nachiketa

remained totally mute. Not a recreant child in the least, he saw to it fit to deliver to his father what was expected of him as a pious and filial son—the noble duty of fidelity and obedience.

Undoubtedly petrified to death, this was for Nachiketa a rude awakening—the unassuming lad having no inkling his father would do something quite this clandestine and cold-blooded. He was reproved and chided to go—for whom now it was a moment of truth.

What a precarious and perilous situation he had suddenly found himself in! But isn't it true that adversity brings out the genius in a man? Showing his debonair spirit, the daring one proved yet another important dictum correct: "Necessity is the mother of invention."

Unlike some moribund lad of his age, this intrepid and audacious son descended unto the Land of Death. Expatriated and ostracized by his father, he went to Yama on a mission duty-bound—determined to uncover the most concealed and dissembled secrets of all.

Here's that truly suspenseful and riveting dialogue that took place between the excommunicated Nachiketa and god Yama. And though he had undue influence over him, Yama never for one moment asserted any of his powers. Rather, under his tutelage the importunate young man was successful in his bid in bringing home the prized secret he betted his life on.

Here's a portion of that beautiful dialogue.

THE DIALOGUE

Nachiketa
> *When a man dies, there arises this doubt:*
> *"He still exists" —maintain some.*
> *"He does not" —insist others.*

> Teach me the truth,
> O King of Death.

Yama

> This doubt haunted even the gods of old,
> for the secret of death is hard to know.
> Do not compel me, Nachiketa.
> Ask some other boons.

Nachiketa

> This doubt haunted the gods of old;
> it's hard to know as you say.
> I can have no greater teacher than you;
> and there is no boon equal to this!

Yama

> Ask rather for sons and many grandsons
> each living a hundred years or more.
> Ask for cattle, horses, gold and vast land.
> Live in good health for as long as you wish.
> Or, ask for whatever else you may so desire.
> Be king over this vast earth, Nachiketa!.
> I will grant you unlimited pleasures,
> unseen and so hard to come by:
> Celestial women rarely seen on earth
> riding in chariots and skilled in music.
> They will attend on you—you may enjoy their love
> as long as you don't ask about death.

Nachiketa

> These pleasures last but until tomorrow;
> and they wear out the vital powers of life.
> How fleeting is all of life on earth, O Death!
> Keep everything—they are yours to enjoy solely.
> Never can man be made happy by wealth.

How can he desire wealth when he meets you—
knows that he cannot live when you are around?
Having met an immortal like you,
how can I, subjected still to old age and death,
ever rejoice in long life?
Dispel this doubt of mine, O King of Death!
This is the boon I choose and ask of you.
Does man live after death—or does he not?

Tested and proven worthy, Yama most pleasingly imparted this most closely guarded secret of his unto Nachiketa. And in amuch didactic manner, Yama pontificated as follows:

Yama

The good and the pleasant,
both of which differ in purpose,
prompt human action.
Those who choose the good attain abiding joy.
Whereas those who choice the pleasant
fail to reach the goal of life.
Perennial joy or passing pleasure—
this is the choice we're faced with.
The wise recognize these choices
but not the ignorant.
The first seeks what leads to joy-abiding,
even though painful in its pursuit.
The latter, goaded by their senses,
run after what seems immediate pleasure.
You have renounced passing pleasures
so dear to the senses, Nachiketa.
You've turned your back on the ways of the world—
that which makes man forget the Goal of Life.
Far apart are wisdom and ignorance.
The former leads to Self-realization—

the latter makes one stranged from the Self.
I regard you, as being worthy of instruction
for fleeting pleasures tempt you not.
Unaware of their ignorance,
but yet wise in their own self esteem,
these deluded men of vain learning
go around the Cycle of Birth and Death—
just like the blind being led by the blind!
"There is this world only—nothing beyond.
When my body dies, I die also."
Thus they fall life-after-life under my sway.
Few ever heard about the Self (the soul)—
still fewer devote their lives to its realization.
Wonderful are they who speak of the Self—
rare are they who make it their supreme goal.
Blessed are they who attain Self or God-realization
through the instructions of an illumined teacher.

*   *   *

With all its arguments and reasoning,
the intellect can never reach the Self—
for subtler than the subtlest is the Self.
Knowledge of the Self does not come
through logic and scholarship, but,
through contact with a Realized teacher.
Dear are you Nachiketa for you
seek the eternal Self.
May we have more seekers like you!

Nachiketa
I know that earthly treasures are transient,
and never can I reach the Eternal through them.
I have renounced impermanent earthly treasures

to win the Eternal through your instructions.
I can have no better teacher than you!

Yama

> *I have availed you Nachiketa*
> *fulfillment of all worldly desires—*
> *power to dominate the earth.*
> *Yet for all you overlooked them all*
> *by application of will and wisdom.*
> *The wise, having realized through meditation*
> *that the timeless Self is difficult to behold*
> *shun pleasures and pain.*
> *The man who realizes that he is his own divine Self*
> *finds the source of all joy—lives in joy-abiding.*
> *I see the gates of joy opening up for you, Nachiketa!*

*   *   *

Nachiketa

> *That which you see as beyond right and wrong,*
> *beyond cause and effect, past and present,*
> *teach me that.*

Yama

> *First, a word about that primeval word.*
> *That word is Om.*
> *That word is the highest.*
> *That word is God.*
> *By repeating this supreme word*
> *one finds fulfillment to all deep longings.*
> *It brings the greatest good to the seeker.*
> *When Om reverberates within the heart*
> *the aspirant feels blessed and deeply loved.*

*   *   *

The all-knowing Self was never born—
nor will it die also.
Beyond cause and effect,
the Self is eternal and immutable.
When the body dies, the Self dies not.
If the slayer believes he can slay,
or the slain believes he is slain,
neither knows the truth.
The eternal slays not—
nor is it ever slain.
Hidden in the heart of every creature is the Self—
smaller than the smallest, greater than the greatest.
They who still the senses are beyond sorrow.
And they behold the glory of the Self
through the grace of the Lord of unsullied Love.
Although a sage sits still for meditation,
the Self exercises its influence far away.
Though stationary, the Self moves everywhere.
When the wise realizes the Self,
Supreme and Omnipresent,
formless in the midst of forms,
unchanging in the midst o change,
they go beyond all sorrows.
Not by the study of scriptures nor intellect
can the Self be made known.
Only to those who the Self chooses
unto him alone the Self reveals itself.
The Self cannot be realized by him
who desists not from unrighteous ways,
fails in concentration or is not at peace—
still not the mind in meditation.

*   *   *

Know the Self as the Lord of the Chariot,
the body as the chariot itself,

the discriminating intellect as the charioteer,
and the mind as the reins.
The senses, say the wise, are the horses;
and selfish desires are the roads they travel.
When a person lacks discrimination
and the mind remains untrained,
the senses run out of control like wild horses.
And instead of reaching the pure state of immortality,
they wander from death-to-death.
Whereas those who possess discrimination
and has a still mind and pure heart,
they reach journey's end—
never again having to fall into the jaws of death!
They attain the supreme Goal of Life—
become united with the God of Love.

Take the last lines of Yama deliberations for example: "They attain the supreme Goal of Life—become united with the God of Love." He made it abundantly clear that Self or God-realization is the objective of life—the process whereby the individual soul becomes one with the Universal soul.

❋ *Eight* ❋

The Building Blocks

THE BRAVE OLD WORLD

WE shall now enter the brave old world of the rishis. And though monumental and Himalayan in nature, our task here would be to find out just how they were able to discover the sublime truth surrounding the mystery of life and death—a question that has foiled and baffled the most brilliant of minds.

Peering through the secret caves of the rishis hearts, we shall rely on the Dialogue with Death and *Gita* as our principal guides. And these, along with the Upanishads and *Bible,* shall serve as the main texts of reference.

Please bear with me as I walk you through this chapter highlighting some of the more important principles introduced by Yama. And we shall take into account also other concepts not considered before but deemed necessary in forming part of the foundation upon which we intend to build our premise.

MAKING TRAVEL PLANS

At any given moment we could easily be snatched away by the cold hands of death ever so eagerly waiting to take a-hold of us. Just like a piece of thread, man's life can be cutoff quite effortlessly—truncated without notice.

And since life is so narrow, petty and quickly ending, why not concentrate all of our efforts to escape it once and for all. Why bury, fudge or have the issue swept under the rug—knowing fully well that the Messenger of Death would fail not paying us that visit one day. Be put on a state of high alert when sounds the knell—be ready, willing and able to answer the door when tolls the bell.

It's like going on a trip. Before embarking upon it, one would enter into the making of elaborate plans and preparations. And the more thoughts one puts into it, the more rewarding the trip turns out to be—the enjoyment being inversely proportional to the efforts expended.

Or it's like pursuing a course of study. If by dint of hard work you happen to master the subject, there would be no fear or jitters come final exam. Then having to face the instructor would be such a delightful moment for you—but not if you had done poorly.

And the same is also true in real life situation. If you live a life of distinction, then the task of having to face the Maker one day would be pleasant. It would be one of great hope—but not if you fail to measure up to expectations.

Conquering death means mastering the *Art of Living*. Therefore, man should go ahead full blast or tilt in propulsion thereto—have in place the required infrastructure. The denouement or solving of the mystery of death is contingent upon us doing just that—pave the way by leading a good and incorruptible life.

THE TWO DESTINATIONS

As purported by the doctrine of *existentialism,* God has given man the freedom to pursue his own path in life— the laxity to take any freeway he so chooses. But though

a free world, Yama advised us that there are two principal pathways to choose from—both of which are like
roads that run in the opposite directions:

The first path leads to what is pleasant—*preya.*

The second path leads to what is beneficial—*shreya.*

PREYA (PASSING PLEASURE)

> *"You cannot worship God*
> *and mammon at the same time."*
> —*The Holy Bible*

Derived from a Sanskrit word, *preya* stands for *passing
pleasure*—the *nine days wonders* really speaking. It titillates
and tantalizes the bumptious ego—whet the appetite so-
to-speak. And some of the real culprits are: aggrandize-
ment, gratification of the senses, appetence, promiscuity,
cupidity, prurience, lasciviousness, licentiousness.

Sounds tempting all right! But the only hitch with our
dissolute and unsavory partner *preya* is that it is momen-
tarily short-lived. Like a dream, it sooner or later fades
away—ever so fleeting, transitory and volatile in nature.

It goes on an errand that delivers you to *fools' paradise*
—a destination liked by no one. It's the lethal path that
leads to confounded ignorance and darkness—having
made mention of which, man ought to be cautioned from
the onset to set sail in the obliquely opposite direction.

All the pleasures and wealth of the world combined
cannot satiate the inappeasable human craving. Man's
gloating and fastidious nature is of such that he is not
gratified even if the entire world is placed at his command
or disposal—for he who so indulges in sensuality or loves
money shall never have enough of it.

As exemplified in the lives of the sybarite and hedonis-
tic ones, never can man be made happy by what is secu-

lar. Hankering after worldly pleasures like mirages, man insatiability can never be quenched—gets only more additive and wedded if anything at all.

Warned the contemporaneous spiritual saint of our times Swami Pranavanadaji Maharaj, "mad indeed is he who thinks that he can unravel the mysteries of a spiritual life with the senses torn by passions—the mind agonized by carnal hankerings."

Sensory pleasures deplete our vital powers of life. It enervates and vitiates our much crucial energy—engenders depression too. And this in further attrition thereto is aggravated by overindulgence in promiscuity and other suchlike degenerative acts mentioned hereinbefore.

When *prana* (the Sanskrit word for "vitality") is overdrawn, there is this sorrowful dullness and sickly pallor overshadowing the whole of ones personality—in exasperation whereof a deleterious array of events set in the life of the haggard looking one: the countenance loses its luster, the eyes their glow, the skin its sheen, the voice its sweet resonance—a profligacy that leaves much to be desired.

How pitiful it is that we seem to live in a world where *preya* exists in plenitude, which, epigrammatically speaking, is the heartthrob and object of infatuation! Its what the world is governed by—in sobriety whereof the globe-trotter gads about in search of pleasure and enticement of the senses.

SHREYA (PERENNIAL JOY)

In the case of *shreya,* the reverse is true. Being the puritanical and salubrious path, its the better of the two—the one recommended by Yama. Its itinerary takes you where you want to go, and its benefits are seemingly endless: It promotes health and well being, invigorates ones vitality,

enhances spirituality, gives everlasting peace of mind—
leads to the light of wisdom.

But like most things beneficial to us in life, there is an
honorarium or price to pay—an investment to make. And
a good example is bodybuilding! One has to labor long
and hard before any results can be seen or felt. Though
unpleasant at first, its benefits stay with you.

Summing up the two pathways then, may we be reminded of Yama's far-reaching words. When prompted
by the enterprising Nachiketa, here's what he had to say.
And as you would imagine, he was being particularly harsh
on *preya* all the way through his deliberations—urged
the misguided human race to hoist sail for the diametri-
cally opposite shore.

Nachiketa
> *These pleasures last but until tomorrow,*
> *and they wear out the vital powers of life.*
> *Never can man be made happy by wealth!*

Yama
> *Perennial joy or passing pleasure—*
> *this is the choice we are faced with.*
> *The wise recognize these choices*
> *but not the ignorant.*
> *The wise seeks perpetual joy*
> *even though painful in its pursuit.*
> *The ignorant, goaded by the senses,*
> *run after what is immediate pleasure.*
> *You have renounced passing pleasures*
> *so dear to the senses, Nachiketa.*
> *You turned your back on the ways of the world —*
> *that which makes one forget the goal of life.*
> *The immature run after sense-pleasures*

and fall right into the widespread Net of Death.
But the wise, knowing the Self to be deathless,
seek not the changeless in the World of Change.

LANDING THE SHORES OF MISERY

Trying to keep our train of thoughts, here're some wonderful teachings on this very topic: Choosing the right path in life sought after by man. Following his own whims and fancies, man in abeyance thereto has been continuously going against the behest of the Lord.

By disobeying Him in eating the forbidden fruit even though duly warned not to, a curse in derision and aberration thereto was pronounced on the reprobate Adam. Showing such a flagrant or blatant disregard for the Lord, he, in contumacy thereto, was held in contempt for which no reprieve was granted.

Even thought what he did might have been out of sheer wanton insolence on his part, punitive measures were nonetheless meted out unto him. And in so doing, the Lord arbitrarily reprimanded and repudiated the accursed Adam.

Thus castigating him, the Lord spoke in much virulent and acrimonious terms. And He had done so with the hope that it would set a precedence—serve as a deterrent to all mankind to come. And being not an innuendo as such, He came downright hard in His reprisal:

"Because you listen to your wife
and ate the fruit,
when I told you not to,
I have placed a curse upon the soil.
All your life you will struggle
to extract a living from it.
It will grow thorns and thistles for you—

you will eat its grasses.
All your life you will sweat to master it —
until your dying day."

—The Bible

Not condoning any of it, God considered it an act of connivance and concoction—took an affront to what they did. Electing to move on a collusion course with the Lord, they had to bear the dire consequences of this karmic wrong—a conviction that has exacerbated and made matters worst for us all.

In exasperation thereto, it should come to us as no surprise at all that even the pleasures sought by man is bereft of its sweetness. And this is due to the stigma and malediction placed upon our lives by the Lord in abhorrence thereto.

In acquiescence and approbation to what has already been declared in the *Holy Bible*, the Paradigmatic Lord Sri Krishna also spoke in augmentative terms. Like His counterpart Yama, He enjoined us to take strong, prohibitive measures against *Preya*:

"You find yourself in a transient and joyless world.
Turn from it and take your delight in me.
Fill your heart and mind with me—adore me.
Direct all your acts of offerings to me.
Bow down to me in self-surrender.
If you set your heart upon me thus,
and take me for your ideal above all else,
you will undoubtedly come to my Being.
Wanting to escape from the fear of old age and death,
men take refuge in me alone."

MISTAKEN IDENTITY

"There is this world only—nothing beyond.
When my body dies, I die also!

> *Thinking like this,*
> *man falls life-after-life under my sway."*
>
> —*Yama*

In their endeavor to enlist the vital components that go into the make up of man, the rishis have readily deciphered that the physical body is made up of five composite, gross elements namely: *earth, water, fire, air,* and *ether.*

By this simplistic way of looking at our bodies, it implies that we are no more than a compostable chemical compound. Made up solely of this inert admixture of biodegradable and combustible materials, it is understandable that man sees himself no more a lump of flesh, easily reducible to a bare handful or cloud of ashes.

Looking at it from this narrow and parochial manner makes perfect sense to us men of indeterminate minds— a similitude we can all comfortably relate to. But this is not to be where the artistry of the rishis were concerned —men who were considered wizards in field of spirituality.

Grown malcontent and uneasy over this pathetic state of affairs, the rishis in recusant thereto refused to subscribe to such a philosophy—the idea that we are a mechanical mold that one day can be reproduced in the laboratory like any other patented drug.

This "identity crises" has caused man to recede backwards—his life became impeded and purposelessly unhopeful. Finding himself more and more alienated and estranged from his higher Self, he has afflictively fallen by the way side—became victim to what is known as *mistaken identity.*

Being unable to salvage and extricate himself from this myopic and purblind state of malfeasance, it is reputedly the most grievous mistake committed by man. What a dereliction and crying shame to beset the maladroit human race!

Placed in this caricature state of discomfiture and disarray, man has been traveling life incognito—and falsely so too as well. But why are we caught in this putative, pseudonymous state? Surely, it must also elicits the sympathy of the pantheon gods to see us placed in this catastrophe or fiasco.

Creating an insurmountable barrier for himself, man in atrophy stands helplessly watching his life evaporating and frittering away. Evasive as it is, this imposition on our lives can be traced right back to that phantasmal monomania—*maya* or delusion.

Casting its magic spell on us, this simulation leaves us feeling disillusioned, overwhelmed and bewildered all at the same time—lost in this agglomerate mass of confusion. And it is not just a mere figment of our imagination either, since this dyslexia distorts our power of vision—renders us totally incompetent to see though the inextricable maze of its illusive structure.

Caught in this labyrinth of deception, we no longer seem to know *who* or *what* we are. And in this rather subversive state we often philander (flirt around) with the obvious question: Am I just this temporal fuselage—a tent that can be easily taken down in a moment's notice? Or am I something more tangible, substantial, palpable—something more tactile and abiding?

Thus questioning, the befuddled man is unable to distinguish between what is *real* and what is not. Though impermanent, one is more infatuated with the corporeal body of his—one he tenaciously clings on and attends as if nothing else matters. Such an appalling *esprit de corpse* (loyalty) one has for the body.

Though everlasting, the soul ends up with the short end of the stick—is neglected at the expense of the body.

And because of this contortion and juxtaposition, it is easy to understand why the body supplants, supersedes and takes precedence over the soul. Why, though superior, it remains the unknown quantity in the equation.

Again, what a woeful plight and quandary to be in—such an unspeakable and cataclysmic disorder to infest the life of man. And brought into such disrepute, it can be amusingly termed the *Walk of Shame*. Thought the strongest link, it is pathetically made the weakest—likened unto giving a dog a bad name.

Displaying such symptomatic decadence and depredation, man's life unbecomingly gets derogated to a lesser status. And finding himself in this muddled and obscured position, he is precluded from knowing his own true godly self—in further relegation whereof he lamentably sees himself just as his mortal coil.

Don't we all suffer also from what is referred to as the *multiple personality syndrome*—a state whereby we assume different roles depending upon the part in life we called upon to play: Be it that of a father, son, brother or our true professional selves, which, in verity thereof, we are none of these.

If left untreated, the prognosis doesn't look good. Therefore, we must find a way out of this attenuated, contemptible state. We must deliver ourselves from the culpable negligence—this astigmatic and sinister position. Let's make a concerted effort to wake up to our true identity—redress matters by taking the necessary remedial actions.

The first thing needs done in certitude is to have ones thinking reoriented—eviscerated and completely rewired. Man must get rid of this inferiority complex—come to the realization that what he is really is the soul: That the soul simply masks or cloaks itself in the raiment or tenement of the physical body—the body being no more a vehicle that carries the soul hither and thither.

Instead of holding oneself out to be the body that happens to have a soul, why not look at it as the soul that occasions a body. Let your sole goal be to reach out for the soul. Mind not the body but the spirit! It is what you are—which by chance only has donned this physical experience in form of the subordinate body.

Granted a seemingly cumbersome arrangement, the soul is camouflaged by the body—the latter being just an instrument of the former. And failing to tap into this dynamic reservoir or fountainhead of empowerment, the soul-force-field, man in atrophy has been reduced to such frugal weaklings—a babe in the arm.

Wouldn't it be a laudable idea if we were to dissever, take leave and part company with the body? Its nothing to brood over too, since man could easily befriend the more permanent and reliable of the two. And it's one form of apartheid that would be met with anyone's full approval.

THE SILENT WITNESS

Attempting to get out of ones cocoon, the germane question now becomes: Since the real *you* is not the body, then what is it really? And as was alluded to above, you are about to hear the same answer repeated in its purest form—this time as it emanated from the lips of the Prescient Lord Himself.

Irrespective of its overall implication or complexity, Sri Krishna disentangled and unraveled it all for us. Unable to measure or guesstimate his lyrical depths, here's an avalanche of much implied, indiscernible knowledge. Referring to his astronomical and augmented presence as *prakriti,* he made this incredible declaration:

"My prakriti is of an eightfold composition: Earth, water, fire, air, ether, mind, intellect, and ego."

Whereas the Physical Body is comprised of the first five elements (earth, water, fire, air, and ether), the Subtle Body is made up of the remaining three (the mind, intellect and ego). We shall expand more on the Subtle Body a bit later on. But for now, I urge you to make a mental note of this all-important eightfold composition.

> *"You must understand that behind this,*
> *and distinct from it,*
> *is the Principle of Consciousness.*
> *It is the source of life in all—*
> *that which sustains the universe too!"*

Behind and distinct from this eightfold composition is that which is the Principle of Consciousness in all beings. What else could this be but the God in man in form of the spirit or soul!

Tautologically speaking then, it appears as if man is comprised of three separate entities: The Physical Body, Subtle Body and the Soul (the Self). But seeing that the Subtle Body and soul are so closely juxtaposed, we often speak of man's dichotomy only—the body and soul.

In the Upanishads, there is a beautiful passage that offers a conciliatory point of view. It tells of the subtle difference between the body and quiescent Self—the latter being the *silent witness* that calmly looks on as we indulge and/or bear the brunt of suffering.

Concomitantly existing together then, we have:

1. The Body: Made of material substances—woven of clay.
2. The Soul: The silent witness—Brahman or God.

Swetasvatara Upanishad mentions these superb verses:

> *Thou Brahman Immortal,*
> *and thou woven of clay —*

two inseparable companions:
Like two beautiful birds of golden plumage,
perched high up on the selfsame tree.
As man, thou tastest the fruits of the tree —
the sweet and sour.
But as Brahman, thou remainest immobile —
though calmly observing.
Forgetting ones oneness with God,
bewildered by his weaknesses,
man becomes full of sorrow.
But he who look closely
sees Thee as Himself —
Lord most worshipful.
And thus beholding God's glory,
lo, all his heavy burdens are turned to joy!

"Thou Brahman Immortal" means you are what God is made-of in form of the soul. And "thou woven of clay" refers to the physical body that is made up of the five gross elements mentioned a moment ago—like two birds of golden plumage yet one inseparable companion.

Thinking that he is the physical body, man has tragically grown aloof of his true godly Self. And in so doing, he becomes susceptible to the ravages of life—looses out on the foremost reason of him being here.

But in antithesis, he who sees the real *you* as the Self and not the body knows that the soul is in no way different from the Lord. And if man were to only accept the fact that he is indeed so blessed, lo, all of his heavy burdens and sorrows shall forever vanish.

So beautifully put, and in such moving tones too, spoke the rishis—words like a beacon light unto a faltering generation of lost souls. And with the veil or scale of ignorance now supposedly falling, may we never again have to doubt our true deiform and angelic sameness.

BRAHMAN

Lord Krishna hereinbefore spoke of the *Atman* (the Self or Silent Witness) as being the vital part of man. Now he is about to intimate to us again that it is also tantamount (one and the same) as Brahman or God—the One Abiding Reality found in every living creature.

Cognizant of this fact, it is contented that man should direct his full attention towards realization of the Self— consider all other endeavors in life irrelevant and distracting. And in demonstration of such repugnance, the sapient and unworldly rishis became resentful or loathsome to all things perishable—took an umbrage and aversion towards them!

As one heedlessly walks pass a golden treasure buried under his feet, so too all beings live in the presence of Brahman. And this form of inconspicuousness (protective concealment) is primarily due to the veil of illusion by which it is cloaked and enshrouded.

But, he who sees God in all, and, all in God, is on his way to realize the Self. And having come to this realization, one is begrudgingly well positioned in his life— reaches the point where God, wanting man to become like him, entered and became part of him.

And in a most befitting and aptly manner, the Lord unequivocally states as follows:

"I am the Self seated in the hearts of all.
Part of myself is the God within every creature.
I am Brahman within this body—
life Immortal that shall not perish.
He who sees himself in all, and all in himself,
helps one to realize the Self oneself.
Brahman is without beginning—
the individual Self mistakenly identified.

> *It is also known as the Silent Winess—*
> *the infinite and supreme Atman!"*
>
> —*The Gita*

THE CHARIOT AND THE TRAVELER

To help us make this important differentiation between the body and Self, Yama likened the body unto a chariot drawn by five rumbustious and unruly horses. And by way of illustration, he drew this wonderful comparison. He compared:

1. The chariot to the body.
2. The five horses to the five senses.
3. The reins to the mind.
4. The charioteer to the discriminating intellect.
5. The passenger to the Self—the one calmly riding along.
6. The roads on which they travel to the sense-objects.

Like our unbridled and mutinous senses, these flying horses are raring to go—gallop from birth to death on the road of desires. And if left to their own free will, they will take the "psychopath" in a hurry to the destination loved best—unquestionably to the self-destructing pathway of *preya* or pleasure.

Here, instead of having the charioteer making the decisions, we end up in a chaotic situation where the horses do—a mass hysteria if you want to put it that way! But just as the horses are under the command of a driver, so too the undisciplined senses fall under the spell of our mind and intellect (*buddhi*).

However, when all is well, the Self makes every decision. They are in turn conveyed by the intellect to the mind. And being the gateway to the mind, the senses are made to submit to it—after which man can be rest assured he would be taken safely to journey's end.

But in order to ensure this happens, we first have to take a good grasp at the unrestrained senses, which, like wild horses, can be trained and made subservient thereto. And just as a charioteer holds back his restive horses, similarly a persevering aspirant can take firm control of the senses—which must be brought at his service!

Our intellect occupies the seat of paramount importance here. But so that it may do its job properly, it needs the full cooperation of the mind and senses. Imagine for a moment having them all pulling their weight together under the influence of a clear intellect holding the reins.

Like the Mighty Buddha, one has to labor long and hard to bring the mind under the firmest of control— who by exertion of both flesh and spirit was adventitiously placed to realize the prized goal of his life! It is only with this type of resolve in mind that the Self-luminous Lord shall be revealed from within.

Here's that amazing analogy Yama presented before:

> *"Now the Self as Lord of the Chariot,*
> *the body as the chariot itself,*
> *the discriminating intellect as the charioteer,*
> *and the mind as the reins.*
> *The senses, say the wise, are the horses—*
> *selfish desires are the roads on which they travel.*
> *When a person lacks discrimination*
> *and the mind remains untrained,*
> *the senses run out of control like wild horses.*
> *And instead of reaching the pure state of immortality,*
> *they wander from death-to-death.*
> *Whereas those who obey the Self,*
> *has a still mind and pure heart,*
> *they reach journey]s end—*
> *never again having to fall into the jaws of death.*
> *They attain the supreme goal of life—*
> *become united with the God of Love!"*

THE MIND WRECKS HAVOC

In seeking the higher Self, we have to make a genuine effort to train our undeveloped minds to grasp higher spiritual truths. Being so vital, we now turn our attention to the psychology or art of controlling the mind. And though difficult, our objective here would be to attain mastery over it.

Speaking of the breviary and compendious *Gita* as being the crystallization of knowledge, let's now carefully examine these measured words uttered by the greatest of all psychologists. Mindful of Arjuna's entreaties, Lord Krishna made himself perspicuously clear in this remunerative colloquy:

Arjuna
Restless and strongly shaken in the grip of the senses,
man's mind is grown hard with worldly desires.
How shall he tame it—the wind is no wilder!

Sri Krishna
Yes, Arjuna, the mind is restless and hard to subdue.
But it can be brought under control by
the constant practice of spiritual discrimination—
the exercising of dispassion.
Never can a man know peace who stirs up his own lust.
Only he who relinquishes lust and desire is so privileged —
him in whom there is no craving for what's mundane.
Though water continuously flow into the ocean,
it is never disturbed nor ruffled by it.
And similarly so too, desires enter into the Seer's mind,
but yet-for-all he is never influenced by them.
Smoke hides fire, dust a mirror, womb the embryo—
and so too the Atman (the soul) is hidden by lust!

Therefore, Arjuna, take control of your senses
and kill this evil thing in the form of lust—
the one obstructing discriminative knowledge
and realization of the Atman or Self.

*   *   *

Thinking about sense-objects,
you become deluded and lustful;
grown attached, you get addicted;
thwart addiction, it turns into anger;
get angry, you confuse the mind;
confuse the mind, you loose discrimination—
loosing which you miss the purpose of life.
As the tempestuous wind turns the ship
from its course upon the waters,
soo too the senses and mind casting adrift,
turns one's better judgment from its normalcy.
The senses are superior to the sense objects,
the mind over the senses—the will above the mind.
And higher than the will is the supreme Atman.
Therefore, Arjuna, exert control over the senses
and mind by the power of the intelligent will!

mmThe sublimed and weighty words of the Lord well delivered indeed. He went to great lengths in acquainting us about concupiscence—the lascivious nature in man that incites lust. And as you would recall, this is no more an extension of our prior discourse on *preya*.

With witticism and logic too, the Lord presented us with this non-argumentative and discursive recapitulation: "Focusing your attention on sense-objects, you become attached; grown attached, you get addicted; thwart your addiction, it turns into anger; get angry, you confuse the mind; confuse the mind, you forget life's most valuable lessons—forgetting which cause you to deviate from the right course."

A convoluted and deranged mind can wreck havoc. And here we see how well the Lord equates and prioritizes it all: "The senses are above sense-objects, the mind above the senses, the will over the mind—but that which is above all else is the dominant and sovereign Self."

First gain control over the debauch and depraved mind by the exercising of dispassion—the practicing of spiritual discrimination. Then with such doggedness and tenacity of purpose, one must perseveringly marshal his way through—bulldoze this elusive enemy that wears the crown in form of lust.

HOW TO CONTROL THE MIND

*"Within you there is a stillness and sanctuary
to which you can retreat and be yourself."*
—Hermann Hesses Siddhartha

Given the plexus nature of the pilfering and remonstrative senses, they perforce engage in a strangulation and tantrum process with the mind. And it's not just a mere war-of-words either, since they seek to trample upon us—the mind itself being a wonderful servant but a terrible master.

Assuaging, tempering, quietening the intractable and dissipated senses and mind fall right within the forte of the much admirable rishis. And when the Lord hereinbefore spoke about employing the right means, what he was in fact implying was meditation—an application that will in the end enable us to achieve this most difficult of tasks.

Having already covered the fundamentals in one of the proceeding chapters, here is this conspectus gesture. Reiterating his position, Sri Krishna pointed out:

"Certainly, if man has no control
he will find this yoga difficult to master.
But the self-controlled man could,
if only he struggles and uses the right means!
The uncontrolled mind does not guess
that the Atman (soul) is present.
Then how can he meditate?
And without meditation, where is peace—
without peace, where is happiness?
Therefore, Oh Arjuna,
make a habit of practicing meditation
and do not let your mind be distracted;
in this way you will finally come to me."

Wait and see for yourself the important task at hand awaiting the mind. It would be assigned the most difficult job of bringing about the union of souls—our's with that of God's.

PRINCIPLES OF EQUANIMITY

Being so closely tied to mind-control, we shall now extend our discussions a little bit further here to incorporate the general principles of equanimity. Briefly defined, equanimity is the exhibition of steady calmness, temperance and equipoise. Its the stolid and abstemious state whereby the mind comes to rest in complete homeostasis, equilibrium and tranquility—the feeling of inexcitability and anorexia.

As is exemplified in the lives of our imperturbable rishis, it is depicted as the state of serenity, placidity and equability—the sedative yogic outlook of these most efflorescent and enlightened souls. And possessed of such composure and impassivity, these defiant seers even intercepted death.

Falling prey to the sway of the mind, most of us get excited when fortune smiles upon us—frowns when misfortune steps in. This instability comes about when one cuts oneself off the lifeline that connects him to the source of all-empowerment, which, if he were to be so wired, could prevent him falling into a state of mental flux and debility.

It is by the application of the *theory of indifference* and apathy that one could garner mental strength. And by that I mean being able to hold the mind in undistracted contemplation on the *Atman*—take a stronghold and gridlock grip on the mind.

Poising one's mind in equanimity, Sri Krishna expounded:

"That person alone is worthy of immortality
who accepts pain and pleasure alike—
that which comes and goes and is never lasting.
Therefore, unmoved and even tempered,
you must accept everything in complete tranquility.
What God wills, he is content.
Pain follows pleasure, and he is unruffled.
Gain follows loss, and he is indifferent.
The enlightened, Brahman-abiding,
calm-hearted, unbewildered,
are neither elated by what is pleasant
nor saddened by what is unpleasant.
He who is not a source of annoyance to the world,
nor is he offended by the world, that Yogi,
having freed himself from the pairs of opposite
(pain and pleasure, gain and loss, life and death)
surely must consider himself very dear to me.
He intelligently copes with the unexpected.
Unperturbed, he is always prepared for the worse

—is neither vain nor anxious about the result!
Same towards friends and foes,
indifferent to honor and insult,
he is satisfied with what's allotted to him.
Be even tempered, Arjuna,
for it is this evenness of temper
what is meant by yoga."

Holding back nothing from us, the Lord most painstakingly issued such wonderful, subliminal words of advice. And He has done so in order that man may become fully apprised thereof—a noble gesture God affords only the human specimen or model.

GROSS AND SUBTLE BODIES

So that we may better appreciate what transpires at the time of death, we are about to introduce a few other cardinal principles here. So please bear with me as we try to conceptualize these most vital concepts. Then we shall turn our attention over to the soul proper.

Outwardly, it appears as if we have just the Gross or Physical Body to contend with. But, a moment ago, we pinpointed that this is not quite the case. And attesting once again to the acuity of the rishis, they discovered that instead of one, we have been living in a bipartite body—one right inside the other so-to-speak.

The first one corresponds to the overt physical body that needs absolutely no introduction. And just below the surface of bodily consciousness lies the second—referred to in Sanskrit as the *sukshma sharira* or Subtle Body. And this is made up of the *mind, intellect* and *ego.*

But beyond all these is found the resident alien—the one and only supreme, covert Self. So quite apart from ones dichotomous self comprising of the body and soul, we are now learning of a further subdivision here, which, in all fairness to the rishis, is a truly remarkable discovery.

There are, therefore, four consecutive layers that must be unraveled before the soul is revealed—securely shrouded, nestled and embowered by all the rest. And for the sake of clarity, here's the sequence by which they are found:
1. First we have the outermost physical body
2. Then lying just below are the three consecutive layers of the Subtle Body:
   The mind
   Intellect
   Ego
3. And finally comes the nethermost Self or soul

Interestingly, what lies closest to the Self is that vainglorious, inflated ego of ours—the individual sense of *I* and *mine* that gets in the way. And it goes without saying that this make-belief friend and impostor must be impugned. For, it is this subversive ego that will prove itself the most difficult to deal with—reason being it is next to impossible to penetrate, let alone going beyond it.

Attempting a bypass will be met with vigorous opposition. The relentless and egocentric one will offer every ounce of resistance—ever so much engage in sabotage and espionage where the amicable Self is concerned. Wait and see what a war it will wage against us trying to reach the abode of the Self—meaning to demolish the impasse.

But on account of its close association with the body, the soul suffers some of the same contusions as does the body. And its only natural for the soul to feel tied down to matter (the body)—comes to think of itself as having some inert characteristics. It's like being held at ransom by the body—gagged and bound hands and feet in chains.

PRANA—THE BREATH OF LIFE

While Gross Body is made up of matter (the five elements mentioned before) Subtle Body is made up of *prana*—a highly complex and subtle form of energy. And the word *prana* literally means life-force, breath-of-life, vital energy."

Born of the Self, we come into this world charged with sufficient *prana* to last until death. Like man and his shadow, *prana* and the Self are wholly and solely inseparable. And this accounts too for them departing together as a unit at the end of life, as we would see later on.

The human body hums with *prana*. Its the power that is involved in every aspect of our human lives. It sustains the millions of events taking place internally and externally. It is what gives rise to intelligence and consciousness—illumines also the being of man.

When we are awake, *prana* is prevalent in the body. When we are asleep, it is fully withdrawn from the body and senses into the mind. So even though *prana* is still very much present in the circuitry, one no longer sees, speaks, hears, feels, tastes. The senses having been unplugged, Gross Body is in a sense dead to the world.

When it is present, all is well—the heart beats, the lungs breathe, the brain functions. When it is no more, life for all intense and purposes is gone, even though the vital organs may still be intact. Formerly there was this living and vibrant person. Now there's just this comatose and lifeless body.

There couldn't be a better symbol for *prana* other than fire. It is true that where there is an abundance of *prana,* there's also the fire of enthusiasm, vitality, zeal, resoluteness—the indomitable will and strength to focus on the goal of life without being ditched or gouged in any way.

We also know only too well how the body wears down

with age. And not withstanding senility, one may still be endowed with a clear mind, possess sound judgment, has an unshakeable will—all so long as *prana* is still present. But the moment it is gone, vitality comes to an end—and so does too life itself. As light goes out when the power is switched off, so too the body ceases to function when *prana* is no more. Try and make a mental note of *prana* as we shall come back to it when going through the sequences leading to death. At that point we shall learn what finally becomes of *prana*—including, of course the Subtle Body and soul.

❋ *Part Four* ❋

THE SELF SUPREME

Objectives

The Soul
We shall be examining in this chapter arguments in support of the soul—soul-stirring discussions you'll find both gripping and penetrating.

Immortality of the Soul
And by the same token, we shall consider here also the immortality of the soul—soul-elevating and mind-boggling facts you never heard before.

✤ *Nine* ✤

The Soul

"As the skin is the center of touch,
the nose the center of smell,
the tongue the center of taste,
the eyes the center of sight,
the ears the center of hearing—
so for all beings the center is the soul!"

—The Upanishads

WE ought to be reminded that in order to overcome death, we have to first of all cut the nexus of our mistaken identity—stop thinking of the body as the real *you* when in fact it is not. Over and above the body is this concentric, axial and centripetal force—the fulcrum or nuclear Self that supersedes the body in every respect.

And in order to establish the rationality behind the amorphous soul, we shall now table some of the many plausible arguments and evidences in adduction thereto —hoping that you would find them both logical and tenable.

But first we have to come up with a working definition of the soul—the *lord of the manor* as far as the physical body is concerned.

DEFINITION OF THE SOUL

The soul is the constitutive principle of man as distinguished from his body—the vital force that enlivens and animates all lives. And being a spark of the divine, it is regarded as a replica, mirror image and carbon copy of God—congenially displaying the same homogeneity, congeneric and kindred nature. In other words, it is held at par with God given its collotype and liberality to the Over-Soul.

In plain language, the soul is synonymous or compatible to God—homologous and akin to the Universal Soul. And thus coexisting and commingling with God, it is a powerful force to reckon with—that which is inveterately placed at the core of ones being.

THE SOUL CREATIVE ENERGY

We have already established that one of the fundamental assumptions of science is that matter and energy are constant. And following the same premise and line of reasoning, we could safely adduce that the soul also falls within the same definition, in that, it was neither created nor can it be destroyed.

Therefore, it can be further extrapolated that the real *you* (the soul) never did take birth! Mark you, the physical body did, but not the real substance by which it is possessed—the soul that is forever existent. And this brings us to the conclusion then that since the real *you* never took birth, how could it possibly die?

Creation infers an impending state of dissolution. And if in fact the soul or its energy thereof was created, it implies then it will also die one day too—a proven absurdity both from a scientific as well as a scriptural point of view.

When you come to think of it, the body ceases to function the moment the soul departs. It seems then as if the *soul-force-field* is what empowers the body—the life-breath or vital principle that impels it. One thinks, speaks, eats, sleeps, dreams all on account of the soul s energy or *prana*. And the moment it departs, vitality comes to an end, and so does too life itself.

Taking into account the soul and its energy-dynamics, the pertinent question now becomes: What happens to all that generative and perceptible energy that once propelled the body? You mean it simply dissipates into thin air and is forever lost—reduced to a state of nullity or nothingness.

Certainly not from a scientific point of view! Physicists maintain that energy is not only preserved but also perpetuated. And this also coincides with the rishis claim that: "That which energizes and activates the body is nothing but the creative energy of the soul—that which perishes not when the body is."

DEATHLESS SUBSTANCES

Man begins dying the moment he is born. And to prove the point, lets look at the anatomical nature and composition of the human body itself. Made up of approximately 50 trillion cells, scientists tell us that they rapidly die and replace themselves over-and-over again—undergo a steady stream of replacement and proliferation.

They concluded that ninety-eight percent of the atoms in our bodies were not there a year ago. And said to be solid, even the skeleton was not there a few months before. And that means one acquires a new skeleton every so often. It comes and goes lust like that.

The stomach lining practically dies every time one digests food, only to be replaced by new tissues later on. And the same is true also of one's skin, hair, toenails, blood cells—nay every other tissue of the human body for that matter. And the beauty of it all is that nature is recreating for us a whole new body.

Therefore, death must not be viewed with such skepticism and negativity. Why presume death is our enemy when in fact all these cells are dying just in order that we may live—help us preserve our continuity. Death is the means Mother Nature so devises to recharge and replenish everything.

Physicists also tell us that our atoms have been around billions of years now; and have left in them that much more life yet. As a matter-of-fact, they do not die but simply get transformed into another configuration of energy—being that they are a form of transformed energy to begin with!

Since the body is composed of these *deathless* substances that know nothing of extinction, why can't we see ourselves in the very same light too! If simple as they are, the atoms live on, then why not also the much more sophisticated soul of man—that which is beyond any physical reproach whatsoever?

Looking at it from this perspective, death no longer holds much meaning—amounts to no more than a "partial truth." And when all is said and done, the truth of the matter is that man is too complex a creation not to fear any better—makes his existence beyond the tomb a grave assurance.

THE EXISTENCE OF THE SOUL

"I am not my atoms; they come and go.
I am not my thoughts; they come and go.
I am not my ego—my self-image changes.
I am above and beyond these.
I am the Witness, the Interpreter, the Self—
ever so ageless and timeless!"

—The Upanishads

And as purported by the doctrine of *solipsism,* the savant rishis too concluded that at the center of ones existence lies the soul. Its the one and only permanent thing known to exist—that which would continue to exist no matter what happens.

Just as gravitation existed long before its actual discovery, so too it is with the laws that govern the spiritual world. For example, the de facto relationship between the individual spirit and the Father of all spirits was always there. And that would continue to be the case even if all mankind were to become forgetful of that fact.

It is hilarious watching scientists trying to convince us that the body is a self-driven piece of machinery They want us to believe that it runs automatically, without the aid of an experienced driver at the helm. But how can this be?

What they fail to realize is that in order to command this intelligently put-together piece of machinery, it calls for a mind superior to the one it comes equipped with. It is like saying a car shifts gears using only the transmission. Clearly, it takes a driver who knows what he is doing—one who performs the gearshifts to maneuver it around.

Being itself basically matter, the body is considered an absolute mold. And comes with it is a smart technician who moves it around—one who interprets and makes all decisions. And this couldn't be just some 'ghost' inside the machine—sounds more like the all-knowing spirit that takes on this technical job.

THE DIVINE GROUND

As it is the sun's intrinsic nature to shed light, so too the Cosmic Soul (or Brahman) radiates itself as multitudinous conscious beings. And its rays reach us as beams of divine emanation in form of our individual souls.

Let's compare the vast ocean to God, and a single drop of water to the individual soul. And if we were to, it can be scientifically shown that the chemical properties of this tiny drop are similar to that of the entire ocean—comprising of two atoms of hydrogen with one atom of oxygen. And that being the case then, it can be logically argued that the individual soul is no different from God—being itself nothing but individual droplets of consciousness in man.

Hindus categorically affirm that *thou art that*: That the indwelling *Atman* is the same as Brahman—the spark of divinity illuminating the inner-man. Inside each and every one of us is a god in embryo waiting to embody itself—manifest its divine decadency.

Aldous Huxley puts it very nicely: "Man possesses a double nature—the phenomenal ego and an eternal Self—the latter known as the inner-man or spark of divinity, which is of the same or like nature as God. It is possible for a man if he so desires to identify himself with the Supreme Spirit. Man's life here on earth has only one end and purpose: To identify himself with his eternal Self and to come to unitive knowledge of the Divine Ground."

CONTINUITY OF GOD'S HIGHEST CREATION

Here's one of the most convincing arguments that could be advanced in support of the soul's existence. Since nature acts to preserve even the inanimate (seeing that matter cannot be created nor destroyed) then how much more wouldn't it try to preserve the continuity of God's highest manifestation on earth—man.

And even if nature were to dictate otherwise, wouldn't God have a say or a hand in the matter? God dearly loves man. And you can be rest assured that He would make certain no destruction comes his way—save him harmless from visitation of any untoward happening.

TRANSCENDENTAL NATURE

It is rather unfortunate for those of us who doubt the existence of God and the soul. And in the manner in which scientists look at things, they would dispose of anything that is not readily discernible to the senses—provable by scientific method.

But, take for example sonic waves that are being emitted all the time. Would it be justifiable to say they do not exist simply because they cannot be picked up by our naked senses? It would be the most preposterous thing to suggest seeing that they are always present—only that we need a radio receiver to do the job.

Just like sonic waves, the soul is also beyond ordinary sensory receptivity and cognition. Being so abstruse or abstract by nature, there's no scientific way to uncover its subtlety—no way for us to determine its constitutional make-up, attributes, noblesse.

And take fire as another example. Though inherent in rocks, it is not readily manifested until one rock is struck against the other. And in like manner too, the soul is found hidden in the body as fire in rocks, butter in cream, oil in sesame seeds—declared the Holy Upanishads.

SUBTLE ESSENCE

*"Even with its power of rationale and reasoning,
still the intellect cannot reach the Self
for subtler than the subtle is the Self."*
—Yama

Presented below in catechetical format are a couple meaningful dialogues that took place between a curious disciple and informed guru. Taken from the *Chhandogya Upanishad*, I shall like you to note how interestingly the guru imparted spiritual knowledge.

Guru
> *"Bring a fruit of that nyagrodha tree."*

Disciple
> *"Here it is, sir."*

Guru
> *"Break it."*

Disciple
> *"It is broken, sir."*

Guru
> *"What do you see?"*

Disciple
> *"Some seeds, extremely small sir."*

Guru
> *"Break one of them."*

Disciple
> *"It is broken, sir."*

Guru
> *"What do you see?"*

Disciple
> *"Nothing, sir."*

Guru
> *"The subtle essence you do not see;*
> *yet in that is the whole of the nyagrodha tree!*
> *Believe, my son, that which is the subtle essence*
> *in that have all things their existence.*
> *That is the truth.*
> *That is the Self.*
> *And that art thou!"*

* * *

And in this prying and ferret disciple's thirst for knowledge, he beseeched his guru to continue this soul-revealing dialogue.

Disciple
"Please, sir, tell me more about the Self."
Guru
"So be it.
Put this salt in the water
and come to me in the morning."

The disciple did as he was told and showed up the following morning.

Guru
"Sip the water, and tell me how it tastes."
Disciple
"It is salty, sir."
Guru
"Though you seeth not the salt,
you sense its presence by having tasted it.
And similarly Brahman though not visible
is very much so present in ones body!
That which is the subtle essence
in that have all things their existence.
That is the truth.
That is the Self.
And that art thou."

The emphasis here is on the soul being the subtle essence, convincingly illustrated by these two examples cited above. It reminds me of the words of our Vedic seers: "The real you cannot be circumscribed or squeezed into the volume of a body or the span of a lifetime, for subtler than subtle is the Self."

Man can be compared to a plant. The plant grows, flourishes and in the end dies. And what it leaves behind is a seed that produces a new plant. And in the case of man, what outlives him is his *karma*—the aggregate of all his good and bad actions. These go with him in determining his next birth

The Upanishads present it this way:

> *"Like corn man falls.*
> *Like corn he rises up again."*

*   *   *

> *"The fruit perishes*
> *but the seed is full of life."*

SILENCE IS GOLDEN

> *"Be still and know that I am God."*
> —Psalm 46:10

Silence is more significant than speech when it comes to spirituality—a form of *lateral thinking* that holds much limpidity and intelligibility. When asked to define the nature of God, there was a dignified silence coming from the reticent and demure sage. And when pressed for an answer, the words of the taciturn one were but few: "The Absolute is silence!"

Referring to it as a pregnant form of silence, Deepak Chopra elaborated as follows: "Nowadays science has enabled us to tract a thought or intention a micro second after it happens. And even with all the scientific equipment in the world, we still cannot tell where it is coming from. You cannot find the real *you* in your mind or your body because you are simply not there. The real *you* is a non-local field of information trapped in space and time by the body and mind. The space between thoughts is silence. Its is a pregnant silence. It is the real Self."

VOICE OF CONSCIENCE

Here's another thought that readily comes to mind pertaining to the soul. What image does it conjure up in the mind's eye when one speaks of his true inner-gut-feelings? One wonders whether or not there is any connection at all to one's inner being giving rise to such elevated and well guided thoughts.

If you were to ask me, I would say so with all surety. Convinced as I am, I urge you next time when in doubt or having to distinguish between right and wrong, good and bad, you should first try meditating before letting your inner-voice of conscience speaks. You'll be amazed at the answers you come up with.

Thus imputing and programing the mind, your infinite subconscious awareness takes over and comes up with the most unimaginative and intriguing answers. What else could this be but the voice of conscience—the voice of God that is inside all of us.

LIKE GOD DID GOD MAKE MAN

It can be argued that if indeed God made man in His own image and likeness as He said He did (like God did God make man), then man can no more die than God can. It is God's promise unto man; unless, of course, He does not really mean what He says. But wouldn't it be impudent and contemptuous on our part even to suggest such a thing—a brazened profanity and effrontery against the Altruistic Father!

Man is special in the eyes of God for in man there's something special—the soul to which God attaches a lot of importance. And whenever He spoke about the soul, He would resort to the most superfluous language known to mankind—in elocution whereof words such as these are treasured as the very *ornament of speech:*

> *"For a soul is far too precious*
> *to be ransomed by mere earthly wealth.*

*There is not enough of it
in all of earth to buy eternal life—
just to keep one soul out of hell."*
—*The Holy Bible*

RISHIS HALLMARK OF FAME

One of the hallmarks of our veracious and peerless Vedic seers is that in the absence of concrete proof they would elect to meet face-to-face with God—if that's what it takes to determine the truth, the whole truth, and nothing but the truth. They felt that this is the only way to clear the air and give rise to verity and certitude.

And without surmising or having to guess, their modus operandi was to follow certain established criteria in order to establish the truth—employ certain methodology to determine what constitutes the truth. And they are: *scriptural authorities, reasoning* and *personal experience.*

We have already shown that the soul is in conformity with scriptures—fully sanctioned and embraced by them. And as seen hereinbefore also, there are many reasonable, logical and defensible arguments in favor of the soul's existence. So what remains to be seen now is whether or not it could be personally experienced at all.

FACE-TO-FACE ENCOUNTER

The rishis have expostulated and reasoned to themselves that since the soul cannot be perceived by the senses, they simply had to go and find a way to make contact with it. And in this soul-searching expedition and bent state of mind, they did just that.

So the best form of proof a Hindu sage gives about the soul and God is that he has contacted them both. That rather than just merely believing in God or steadfastly holding on unto dogmatic principles, Hindus concern themselves more with realizing, being and becoming like God.

Quite objectively then, Hinduism is a *Way of Life*. It involves man constantly trying to become divine—to reach God, to behold Him, and to be one with Him. And it is this reaching God, seeing God, becoming like God, what constitute the lofty religion of these Vedic seekers of truth.

And in affirmation or verification of the truth, they met vis-à-vis with God—in ratification whereof we shall later on be citing cases of individuals who have achieved this magnificent feat. Under the chapter dealing with *nirvana* we would learn how they not only encountered the divine but ultimately became divine themselves.

✳ *Ten* ✳

Immortality of the Soul

THE ULTIMATE REALITY

Man's dichotomy is comprised of his pseudo-body and the real inner-man he is. And finding it increasingly difficult to accept the fact that the real *you* is not the body, one finds himself in a rather confounded state of existence—his difficulty being unable to distinguish between his seemingly ambivalent or ambiguous nature.

Earlier we considered how one is purposely led astray by the delusive power of *maya*—think of this mendacious body as being the putative *you* when its not. One's personality is no more a shadow cast by the Self. And *maya* is where we mistake the shadow (the body) for that which is real. Such an outlandish state of affairs to plunder the life of man—reduce it to mere shambles.

Whereas to the average man the Self seems shadowy and unreal, the body is viewed quite the opposite—that which for all intense and purposes looks, feels and sounds real. And quite oddly enough then, one pays full attention to the meaningless body at the expense of the meaningful Self—the soul that is made the underdog in this vivid example of reverse discrimination.

Maya deliberately seeks to divert our attention by the vast spectacle of attractions she has so provided. Thus the blindfolded man looses out on the substantive spirit while grasping at the morsel—forsaking the permanent and lofty Self for the insignificant, perishable body.

But why this perpetration of "Self-defeat." It amounts to no lesser a treasonable and perfidious act—the fact that we choose to simply dismiss or underscore the soul. Why must the Self play the supporting role when it should be given the lead one? And in many instances, it's given no role at all.

THEATRE OF CHANGE

This delusive world is a *theatre of change*. And every living thing in the universe suffers the same evanescence: All creatures, animals, plants change and eventually die. And even our bodies, said to be real, it is not exempt from this corrosive nature of things.

Exposed to this constant state of flux, desires, wealth, name and fame also fall within the same category of impermanence. And included in the list also is the much inflated ego of ours.

What good can come out of such possessiveness, inordinate pride and rapacious greed when they are not of an everlasting nature? Considering that nothing lasts forever including our bodies we are so much in love with, then what's the point in us killing ourselves hoarding treasures on earth—for what purpose, for what end really!

Nothing in this world is yours. Not your ego, not your wealth, not your spouse, not even your children. Nay, not a single thing in this whole wide world belongs to you save and except your soul—the one and only notable exception to the rule.

Sidetracting a bit, here's a little philosophical gesture: What have you lost that you cry? What did you bring with you into this world that you have lost? What did you create that got destroyed? Today what is yours was someone else's yesterday—and will be some else's tomorrow.

As is upheld by the *theory of solopism,* the soul is considered the only permanent thing in all of this world. It will exist no matter what happens. And even upon the final dissolution of the world it would not be affected in any way.

Come to think of it, no one possesses the power to kill you. Perhaps your body, but not the real *you* by which you are constituted. Then why worry unnecessarily in vain? And considering the gravity of the situation, words such as these should be indelibly inscribed in the hearts of us all—engraved and etched in letters of gold.

Getting down to the crux of the matter then, only the eternal Self can be viewed in this light—wherefore our first step towards immortality is for us to develop an extreme aversion to all things perishable. Only then would we be able to see through the illusion of change and decay we are surrounded by.

Like Brahman and the soul, what is *real* never changes. Nothing in this phenomenal world, other than Brahman and the soul, can be said to possess ultimate reality. And if paraphrased, it would read something like this: Apart from Brahman and the soul, everything else is subject to change, decay and death.

As the unchanging reality behind the changing universe is Brahman, so too the unchanging reality behind the changing body is the soul. And as declared by the Holy Vedas, the *Atman* (the soul) and Brahman (God) are one and the same. In the hearts of all dwells the Lord—the One Most Effulgent.

THE SOUL'S IMMORTAL NATURE

In the preceding chapter we looked at the soul in circum-

stantial details. We examined the logics or theory behind
its existence. And now in like manner we shall set out to
examine its immortality—the soul that calibrates itself to
take on the human experience.

To derive maximum benefits from the soul-force-field,
we first of all must be cognizant of the fact that we have a
soul. We have to accept the fact that we are indeed so
blessed—possess a soul that is ever so fulsome, inobsolete
and immortal. And this would be the stepping stone or
birth of a new and more vibrant you.

Asseverating his position thereof, Sri Krishna made this
very timely and masterful treatise. Unilaterally declared in
no uncertain or nebulous terms, He gave this very intru-
sive and all-encroaching description of the soul—in elucidation whereof. He spoke in panegyrical and mellifluous
tones gripping the attention of his enamored disciple
Arjuna:

"I am the Self seated in the hearts of all—
the beginning, middle and end of all beings.
That which is non-existent cannot come into being—
and that which 'is' cannot cease to be.
He who knows the innermost reality
knows the nature of 'is' and 'is not'—
that indestructible and unchanging reality
no one on earth has the power to destroy!

*   *   *

Bodies are said to die,
but that which possess them is eternal—
cannot be limited nor diminished in any away.
Some claim the Atman is slain
and others conclude it's the slayer—
both of whom are totally ignorant
since it cannot slay nor be slain.

Know Atman to be:
Indestructible, immutable, changeless,
ageless, birthless, deathless, eternal,
unmanifested, incomprehensible, unceasing,
endless, imperishable, unlimited—
incapable of being burned by fire, dried by wind,
wetted by water, wounded by weapons!
Therefore, how can it die
upon the death of the body?

*   *   *

Worn-out garments are shed by an individual
just as worn-out bodies by the in-dweller!
New bodies are constantly donned,
like garments, by everyone!

*   *   *

Imperceptible to the naked senses,
not comprehended by the mind,
not subjected to modification,
for such are the abiding qualities
of the innermost principle.
Before birth it is not manifested to the senses.
but between birth and death it becomes manifested.
And having to return to the unmanifested state,
then what's there in all of this to grieve over?

*   *   *

Death is certain for the one born
as rebirth is for the dead.
Man is born to die
and die to be reborn again.
Wherefore, the truly wise mourns
not for the living nor the dead—

grieves not for what is unavoidable.
There was never a time when
you nor I did not exist—
nor shall there be a time
when we shall cease to be.
Just as this body is subject
to childhood and old age,
so too at death man merely passes
into another kind of body.
You and I have lived many lives in the past.
And while I remember them all, you don't!"
                                                    —*The Gita*

In such proliferation came the torrential downpour of words as the blessed Lord passionately delivered his *immortal message*—in perpetuation whereof we find his opening statement quite explicit and noteworthy: "I am the Self seated in the hearts of all."

Sri Krishna made it abundantly clear that dismemberment of the body does not in any way affect the soul. Like matter and energy, the soul was not created nor can it be destroyed too. And now you are hearing it from the Lord himself. And mark his words: "That which is nonexistent cannot come into being; and that which 'is' cannot cease to be."

In a superlative, exorbitant and inexhaustible manner, the Lord went to great lengths in describing the soul to be: "Indestructible, immutable, changeless, ageless, birthless, deathless, eternal, unmanifested, incomprehensible, unceasing, endless, imperishable, unlimited—incapable of being burned by fire, dried by wind, wetted by water, wounded by weapons."

Equated with God, for such is the deistic quality and nature of the soul. And you would have to agree with me, he left no stones unturned when He further stated that:

"Death is certain for the one born—rebirth for the dead. That which dwells within all living bodies remains forever indestructible."

And in summing up his position He again reiterated in the end that: "wherefore the truly wise mourns neither for the living nor dead. You and I, Arjuna, have lived many lives in the past. And while I remember them all, you don't."

Having listened with rapped attention to this most exquisite expatiation, Arjuna in the end was left totally speechless—became most enlightened.

FROM A BIBLICAL POINT OF VIEW

Here are a few of the many selected Biblical quotations that firmly support the doctrine of the Immortality of the Soul. These statements may not be as categorical and direct as the ones made by the Lord Sri Krishna, but they nonetheless corroborate and lend support thereto:

"I was dead and yet I live.
Don't be afraid of those
who can kill only your bodies
but can't touch your souls!

*   *   *

Yet not I
but Christ liveth in me.

*   *   *

The gift God gives is everlasting life.

*   *   *

For God loved the world so much
that he gave his only begotten son
so that anyone who believe in him

shall not perish
but have everlasting life.

*   *   *

I am the resurrection and the life.
Whosoever believes in me
even if he dies,
yet shall he live.
And any one who believes in me shall
not die unto the age to come.''

✻ *Part Five* ✻

THE FIRST OF TWO PATHS

Objectives

Having thus learnt from the most authoritative sources there are about the immortal and intrinsic nature of the soul, we are now ready to explore what finally becomes of it upon death of the physical body.

And broadly speaking, there are two pathways the soul traverses after death:

1. The Path that leads to Rebirth or Reincarnation.
2. The Path of No-Return.

We shall examine the first path here before turning our attention over to the second, which, as the title of the book suggests, shall be given greater emphasis. And being the cornerstone upon which we have thus far built this beautiful edifice, *reincarnation* will be looked at again. But this time around, it would be treated from a purely applied and concrete manner.

❋ *Eleven* ❋

The Path that leads to Rebirth or Reincarnation

ADDRESSING Arjuna, the Lord Sri Krishna enunciated the first of the two pathways:

> *"There's two paths to choose from:*
> *The path that leads back to birth*
> *and the path that leads to no-return.*
> *These two paths, the dark and the bright,*
> *have existed from a time without beginning.*
> *The first is the path of night and smoke—*
> *the path of the moon's dark fortnight*
> *and sun's six month's journey to the south.*
> *The person who takes to this path*
> *reaches the lunar light—*
> *the path leading to human birth."*
>
> —*The Gita*

Before examining how one gets to come back to human birth, let's look at what physiological changes take place at the time of death—what process, if any, takes precedence. And having done so, we shall be in a much better position to make some meaningful deductions and generalizations.

SEQUENCES OF DEATH

We begin with this concise account taken from the *Brihad-aranyaka Upanishad*. Here's the full text put into such beautiful prose:

"When a man is about to die,
the Subtel Body, mounted by the intelligent Self,
groans as a heavily laden cart groans under its weight.
When his body becomes emaciated through old age,
the dying man separates himself from his limbs
even as a fig detaches itself from its stalk.
And by the same way he came he hastens back
to assume another body in which to beigin life anew.
Having been rendered totally unconscious,
the dying man gathers his senses about him,
and, after completely withdrawing their powers,
he descends into his heart.
He sees, smells, speaks, hears, feels not.
they organs having been detached,
they become united with Subtle Body.
And at the point of his heart where the nerves join,
it is lit by the light of the Self.
And by this light he departs through the eye
or another aperture of the body.
Thus life departs and all functious
of the vital principle cease.
But the Self remains conscions.
And in this conscious state
man goes to his new abode to begin life anew
—takes with him his karma.

*   *   *

As a leech having reached the end of a blade of grass
draws unto himself another,

so the Self having left the body behing unconscious,
takes hold of another.
As a goldsmith takes an old jewelry and
molds it into a newer, more beautiful piece,
so the Self having left the body behind unconscious
takes on a better from—
that of a celestial singer, a god
or some other beings, heavenly or earthly."

Having already looked at NDE's (near death experiences) we can now draw a striking parallel here. In relating their tales, NDEer's spoke of their feelings of painlessness in this apparently painful situation. And here one could make the very same deductions too.

With the senses completely withdrawn, it makes the body oblivious to the sensations of pain—is rendered fully unconscious. What a relieving and comforting thought this is—the assurance given here that death is made painless.

This is not to say there is no pain at all in death. Prior to death there are, as is generally prevalent in life, but not during the crucial process itself. But doesn't this seem strange that where we expect it most, particularly at the time of death, there's no pain to speak of!

And where we would expect it least, there's so much to behold! Have you ever considered the number of times you've been hurt both physically and emotionally? And if you were to take stock, I am sure you would be absolutely amazed how much of life is underlined with pain!

But even if there's pain during death, it has practically no effect on us seeing that the body is initially made unconscious. It's just like being under anesthesia while a surgeon is amputating your leg. And unlike deep-sleep or dream which death would be later on compared to, one does not have to wake up to face the griming reality of his own demise.

The Upanishads did make mention that of the fact that "the dying person groans as a heavily laden cart would under its weight." But this is prior to death, and not during the critical stages itself. And moreover, this is applicable only in cases of the aged who has grown thin and emaciated. I have witnessed many dying—people and animals alike. But never have I seen any trying to run away and/or offer any violent resistance thereto. There is none of this wailing or gnashing of teeth, ranting and raving— no form of vociferos behaviour whatsoever!

Speaking about *light* also, you've just heard the Lord alluding to lunar light. The rishis have made mentioned of the fact that "lit by light of the Self, it is by this light the soul departs"—pinpointing that all these characteristic associations with light do in fact ratify and lend credibility to NDE's.

Yet another very important point to bear in mind here is the claim made that "at the point of death the luminous Self remains fully conscious; and in this conscious state, the dying person goes to his new abode in which to begin life anew."

This readily brings to mind two things: The first has to do with the inference made to light "the luminous Self." Then comes the startling declaration made pertaining to the fact that "the Self remains conscious" after death.

This seems to prove correct the suspicion I've always had: that it seems as if the deceased is somehow aware of his surroundings—possesses the power of clairvoyance.

PASSPORT

Karma is our passport to the other world. And just as if there were classifications in visas being issued rated according to one's deeds, the highest would get you a permanent visa in the hereafter—reaching which you would not want to have anything to do with coming back to the world left behind.

The second highest would get you a re-entry visa to this world of mortal men—whereas the third would leave you hanging in limbo. And the inference here is that there could very well be some sort of retrogression to a lower status in life—be it that of an animal or some other lowly creature.

If that was what ones biddings were, then so be it! The chips would fall where they may—follow the dictates of *karma*. And in this decrement or diminishing order then, man is impelled by the impressions of his *karma*. He gets out of life precisely what he puts into it, based on the most foolproof, equitable Law of Karma.

The quizzical Arjuna took the opportunity to inquire from the Lord as to what becomes of him who tries hard but yet-for-all fails to reach the enviable goal—referring of course to the path of no-return.

Acceding to his request, the Lord made this "heaven-and-earth" differentiation.

This is how the dialogue unfolded:

Arjuna
"When a man goes astray from Brahman (God)
he misses both lives—the worldly and the spiritual.
Is he not lost as a broken cloud in the sky?
This is the doubt that troubles me.
And only you can remove it altogether.
Please let me hear your answer, O Lord!"

And the Percipient Lord Sri Krishna answered in these most endearing terms:

"No, my son, that man is lost
neither in this nor the next world.

No one who asks his way to Brahman
ever comes to an evil end.
Even if a man fails to achieve the goal,
he, having performed good deeds,
shall win the heavens—
dwell there many long years to come.
Eventually he will be reborn in the home
of pure and prosperous parents,
or even that of an illumined Yogi—
though the latter may be difficult to obtain.
Regaining all of his spiritual discernment
acquired in his former life,
he would strive harder for perfection—
be driven unto union with Brahman.
Thus struggling hard by cleansing oneself,
that yogi will at long last attain perfection."

—*The Gita*

The most reassuring and comforting words of the Lord here serve to remind us that no one who seeks God ever comes to an evil end. He steers the boat of their lives and ensures they never get lost amidst the storm of life—suffer the fate of a broken cloud lost in the sky.

Failing to reach the prized goal does not preclude one winning the heavens—given another opportunity to build on his spiritual discernment earned in preceding births. And thus having this cumulative effect, it would one day culminate in man being fully recompensed in the end.

TRANSMIGRATION OF THE SOUL

In reality then there are three principal pathways:
1. The Path of No-return
2. The Path of Return
3. The Path of Retrogression

Allegorically speaking, we see the same scenario too unfolding itself in the Courts of Law. After listening to ones submissions, the judge would either have the accused acquitted or punished. And so too adjudged by his *karma,* man, failing to obtain a permanent release from this world (referring to the Path of No-return) is sentenced to serve time in one of the other two destinations mentioned above.

The human body is just a vestiture or apparel for the soul. And as seen in the example given before by Yama, the passenger is free to jump aboard another chariot when the one he is riding along breaks down or is declared unfit. He simply abandons it for another.

Based on the *Principles of Transmigration of the Soul,* one enters and exists various bodies as they become uninhabitable. Come to think of it, what's the big deal in all of this—the fact that we have to discard one body for another. It's just like casting-off worn garments for newer and more fashionable ones.

Man willy-nilly goes round-and-round the *Karmic Cycle of Birth and Death* until he attains perfection—failing which he either maintains his position on the wheel or risks being thrown out of its rhythmic pattern. And if in fact he does, his life deteriorates or retrogresses below that of human birth.

The workings of *karma* are of such that man goes to a higher or lower sphere after death. His destiny is either for the better or worst. And should it be the latter, he has absolutely no one to blame but himself. The infallible Law of Karma takes effect.

But luckily for man, from a broad biological point of view, evolution works for the better. It moves towards the higher rather than the lower end of the spectrum—

wherefore we must once again be very thankful to God.

THE SOUL'S JOURNEY

*"As the wind steals perfume from a flower,
so too the soul takes with it
the senses, mind, intellect and ego
when it departs from the body!"*
—The Upanishads

When a man dies he sheds his ephemeral body of flesh and bones—resides thereafter in the Subtle Body comprising of the mind, intellect and ego. And the soul, along with these vital components, survives annihilation of the physical frame.

In the secret reservoir of the mind is stored all impressions of life. And seeing that the mind is an integral part of the Subtle Body, it stands to reason that ones personality does in fact persist after death—does not in any way mark the end of the human existence.

The post-o-bit effect of it all is that right after death, the soul or its energy thereof remains earth bound for a while. And due to its irresistible attraction towards the body, the soul peregrinates or hovers over it during this intervening stage.

So the quicker the body can be disposed of, the better it is for the soul—being the very reason why cremation is preferred over burial. In case of burial there is a greater chance for the soul to remain attached to the body. In cremation, even the remains (ashes) are immersed in water so as to minimize any chance of contact.

Not only cleaner and more hygienic, cremation also expedites the return to their respective abodes the earthy elements by which the body is composed, namely earth, water, fire, air, and ether. *Ashes to ashes, dust to dust*—so we are told. Suddenly it's all beginning to make perfect sense now! Isn't it?

DESIRES MAKE OR BREAK US

If the Subtle Body breeds any desire in the end, life commences all over again. What you are today is the cumulative result of all the desires you've ever had. And the cause of rebirth too can be traced to desires, which, only after they are completely extinguished can man be discharged or emancipated.

According to the nature of one's desires, the appropriate body is formatted—constituted for that purpose. Like a seed, life quickens again into a new body—one scrupulously designed to match the cherished desires.

Inevitably then, desire makes or breaks us. It all has to do with the residuary nature of one's inclinations and wishes. And in attestation thereto, below are some brilliant deductions made by our peerless rishis—sentiments beautifully expressed Shakespearean style: Tell me of your desires (show me your friends) and I will tell you who you're going to be (and I will tell you who you are):

> *"As are his desires so is his will.*
> *As is his will so is his deed.*
> *And as is his deed so is his reward.*
> *Thus he who has desire*
> *continues to be subjected to rebirth.*
> *But in him whom desire is stilled*
> *he suffers no rebirth—ever!"*
> —The Upanishads

✳ *Part Six* ✳

How to Conquer Death

Objectives

Because of its many ramifications, I have broken down this section into two parts even though *nirvana* and the path of no return are one and the same.

The Path of No-return
Having already considered the due processes of death, we shall now examine, among other things, the unique departure route reserved for the soul of the Self-realized person.

Nirvana
Being the state of union with Brahman, *nirvana* will captivate our full attention here.

❊ *Twelve* ❊

The Path of No-return

A FULL DECK OF CARDS

HAVING thus covered the basics, we are now presented with a full deck of cards in the game of life. And if we were to play our cards right, we could come up with a convincing victory over death—the stake for which we are playing.

And in the most befitting manner, we begin to build our conclusive arguments by giving hearing to no other than Yama—the god of death who had already made his overpowering presence felt.

YAMA'S GOLDEN ADVICE

In the battle of life and fight for which we were born, we have been caught napping. And so Yama quite fittingly makes this wake up call:

"Get up! Wake up!
Blessed are they who make Self-realization their goal
which comes not through logic and scholarship
but through guidance of an illumined teacher!
Sharp like a razor's edge is the path—
most difficult to traverse.

And dear are you Nachiketa,
for only one in a million seeks the eternal.
May we have more seekers like you!"

The operative word here is guidance. To cross the ocean of mundane existence, we need the guidance or surveillance of one who knows the way—a worthy navigator, yatchman or guru. And as the proverb has it: *When the pupil is ready the teachers will appear!* And here's those teachers: Yama, the rishis, the blessed Lord Sri Krishna and Jesus.

The redeeming grace of God is also of paramount importance. And the mere fact that you are reading this book is testimony that you are well intentioned—be it even an iota of desire you may be so harboring. Or, you can in the lease breathe a sight of relief that Grace has finally noticed you.

Before you know, you'll be on track to stake your claim for immortality here and now. And having resolutely resolved, there's absolutely no power on earth to stop you any longer. Where there is a will, there is a way. Seek, and ye shall find. Knock, and it shall be opened unto you.

Considering the fact that you have attained this human body speaks copiously or voluminously for you. The body is a raft lent us by God to cross this hypothetical ocean, which no other forms of life is so privileged nor blessed to have.

And here's an appropriate substantiation thereto:

"Rarely do I, thy Lord God,
who loves the jivatman (soul)
ever bestows it upon a human—
the body itself being a veritable raft

to cross the ocean of mundane existence.
And with My grace as a favorable wind
and a worthy guru or teacher as helmsman,
a combination though difficult to secure,
has been made possible on account your good deeds.
And he who thus equipped
still fails to cross the ocean of existence
verily commits the act of Self-slayer!'
—*The Ramayana*

THE SECOND PATH

We have already considered the first path that leads to rebirth. And Lord Sri Krishna shall now describe for us the second path—the one brightly lit and lined with success. And understandably so, it is the one He would like to see us all faithfully treading—the *Northern Lights* as it is commonly referred to.

"The second is the path of light, fire and day.
It's the path of the moon's bright fortnight
and sun's six month's journey to the north
—verily the auspicious path to Brahman.
The Self realized one who takes to this path
goes to Brahman—the point beyond return."

Having thus enunciated the second pathway, lets now look at some other salient points before tackling the most important chapter on *nirvana*. And we begin with these preliminaries and precursory considerations outlined in this broad overview.

BROAD OVERVIEW

Gripped by death, within this mortal body dwells the immortal soul. And when man assumes a close relationship with his body instead of the soul, he becomes enveloped in a world of duality—subjected to the pairs of opposite such as pain and pleasure, gain and loss, life and death.

As long as this misguided situation lasts, he would not be able to find real peace and happiness. And the resultant effect is that the soul will continue to take on a new covering until it reaches the point of ultimate perfection—not until endeth the dance of opposite.

You have undoubtedly heard of the *Sermon on the Mount*. Now listen to the summation of the *Sermon on the Chariot*. Staged on a battlefield, the entire dialogue between Arjuna and Sri Krishna took place on a chariot. And coincidentally too, this chariot was also drawn by five powerful steeds, with no other than the Lord Himself holding the reins as charioteer.

And in the example given before by Yama, we see here now a more revealing and complete picture. Apart from the comparison drawn that likened the body to a chariot, the five horses to the senses, the reins to the mind, the driver to the intellect, in this setting Arjuna is compared to the individual or micro soul, and Sri Krishna to the Universal or Macro Soul.

It should come to us as no surprise at all that so much was spoken about death. Death was the central theme in their discourse. The Lord had to convince the much distraught Arjuna to fight that righteous war—not to renege out of fear of dying and/or causing death.

Like a Moses, he was charged with the responsibility of leading his people to freedom—to regain their lost kingdom usurped at the hands of their unrighteous cousins. And showing signs of cowardice, he was willing to concede victory to them—wanted to shirk from his noble duty as a warrior.

And Sri Krishna had to remove this fear from the mind of the despondent Arjuna—snap him out of the spell of delusion and melancholy by which he was overtaken. Hence, we see now why his mentor Sri Krishna had to plead and reason with him every so often—especially when Arjuna was trying to exculpate and exonerate himself thereof.

Like valiant soldiers stands man on the battlefield of life. And the divine teachings expounded here by the Lord are the conscriptions, ammunitions and armaments of war, needed to combat the impediments of life—a fight we cannot run away from like an escapist as the fugitive Arjuna was trying to do.

In a very protracted manner, the blessed Lord Sri Krishna shall articulate his final decree: *How man is made perfect and one with Brahman*—the goal of wisdom. And urging Arjuna to listen carefully, he presented herein the grand finale of his inciting deliberations—the summation of the *Sermon on the Chariot*.

Showing very little latitude, Sri Krishna casts this magic spell over Arjuna—the one designate to receive this Gnostic Message of Lord. And bringing into play the full magnitude of his oratory and dialectical skills, the Lord expatiated one of the most impassioned messages of all times—an interlocution or expostulation second to none:

"Harken, Oh Arjuna!
Now that I have taught you the secrets of secrets
ponder them over carefully and then act as you see fit.
These are the last words that I shall say to you,
the deepest of all truths—the king of knowledge.

I speak for your own good.
You are the friend I choose and love.
Learn from me now
how man, made perfect,
becomes one with Brahman—
the goal of wisdom.
I lay before you the conditions precedent or
deemed necessary for God-realization—
man dwelling united with Brahman:

- **When without regret and aversion, the mind and heart are freed from delusion—will steadied and senses subdued.**
- **When man eats but little and seeks solitude—curbs his speech, mind and body.**
- **When fully engaged in Brahman (the truth), he hates no living creature—is compassionate to all.**
- **When he frees himself from the delusions of I and mine—get rid of the phenomenal ego standing in his way.**
- **When he casts from his mind vanity, pride, lust and anger—rids himself of all material possessions.**
- **When he becomes totally tranquil at heart.**

*   *   *

To love is to know me,
my innermost nature,
the truth that I am—
through which knowledge
one enters at once to my Being.
Have you listened carefully
to everything I have told you, Arjuna?
Have I dispelled the delusions
of your ignorance?

Arjuna

> *By your grace, O Lord,*
> *my delusions are dispelled.*
> *My mind stands firm—*
> *its doubts ended.*
> *I shall now do your biddings!'*

Completely mesmerized by this most fabulous confabulation, it climaxed and ended on a very positive note—left Arjuna practically loss for words. And setting out to make our final submissions, we shall appropriately begin with desire—the cause of all causes. And although reference was already made thereto in the preceding chapter, we would now get into the crux of the matter here.

A FOREST OF DESIRES

> *"In him whom desire is stilled,*
> *he suffers no rebirth."*

*   *   *

> *"When all desires*
> *have been driven out,*
> *the mortal becomes immortal."*
> —The Upanishads

Life begins and ends with desire. It is by our desiring to live that we are in fact dying! And being that it is so 'deadly' in nature, desires harm us beyond the point of recovery—so much so that if at the end there's even a tinge of it, life has to begin all over again.

Man goes round-and-round the Cycle of Birth and Death—until he completely rids himself of all base and abject desires. And it is only when this requirement is fulfilled that man can be freed from the effects of *karma*—

becomes pure enough to enter the unitive state with God. The problem though is that are besieged by an exorbitant amount of desires—a protuberance, surfeit and a barrage of them to combat with. And they cause such a consternation in our lives—a conflagration that could result in us being totally consumed in the end.

Being the root cause of all sufferings, desires very much spell man's ultimate doom. Taken a-hold of us, they grip us ever so strongly—drag us through the hellish cyclical motions of life.

THE WEEDING-OUT PROCESS

As one gets closer to this last frontier called death, he must narrow all choices until there remains standing alone the one pure, driving desire of all of his heart—the residuum desire for Self or God-realization.

In the world of spirituality, selfish and mercenary desires lead to bondage and suffering. And in abatement and attrition thereof, we must first transform all self-seeking and illiberal desires into selfless ones. And these, in turn, must be modified and reduced to the one aforementioned desire.

Since vile desires encumber our lives, they must not only be truncated but altogether stultified and eradicated—the whole shebang and retinue of them. We have to find a way to extirpate this inoperable, malignant cancer. And having to eschew a recrudescence or reflux, every desire must be confronted head-on the moment there's any symptomatic reappearance—nipped in the bud.

WILL POWER

Have no qualms or misgivings about it! Man is a creature

of habits. And we know only too well how habit is difficult to break. Like habits, when one desire sets us free we are chained by several others—speaking of which this chain reaction keeps us forever bound and imprisoned.

No wonder the ancient Greeks cherished it as one of the greatest sayings of all time: "when the gods want to punish us they grant our desires." And here we see why this truly becomes a problem in our hands, reason being that as more desires of ours get fulfilled, the more there are to quell.

Rupturing this chain of events calls for a disciplined mind and an indomitable will—something easier said than done. And seeing there is a myriad of desires eagerly waiting to gobble us up, we have to firmly stand up to them so that we do not become so gullible after all—assailable and defenseless.

Seeking to launch an all out assault against desires, one has to struggle long and hard until the will becomes totally unshakable. And if we don't, desires will attribute a lot of pressure on us. Like a mighty current, they will push us against the tide of our wishes—the feelings you get as if someone is trying to push you off a cliff.

Our thoughts are like seeds that grow and bear fruits in the form of desires. And if we're to sow only positive thoughts in the wide-open field of our consciousness, then the yield shall be the most fruitful of desires—not just some hybrid breed.

EGO AND THE SELF

*"Man is made perfect and one with Brahman
when totally free from the sense of ego—
free himself from the delusion of I and me."*
—*The Gita*

As a result of the vendetta, prolonged feud and loggerhead between our two selves (the love/hate relationship between the lofty Self and the obstreperous ego) there's this constant tug-of-war we're embroiled over.

Whereas the Self wants to sow only seeds that will bear good fruits, the voracious, vindictive and inimical ego evasively seeks to outwit its virtuous opponent. It awaits the opportunity to employ its many devious tactics and foul-play—exerts great force in wanting to accumulate hordes of money, power, name, fame.

Working under such false pretences, the kleptomaniac and egocentric one is interested in promoting its own welfare only—gluttonously seeking the lion's share in everything. And in stark contrast thereto, we have the compromising spirit, full of love, wondering how it can be of help always.

FINAL THOUGHTS

After the Self has gained the upper hand over this "dog in the manger," it then becomes necessary to have our desires merged into the one commanding desire for Self or God-realization. And as you would imagine, there has to be a very good reason why the rishis recommended having this one-tract mind—a protocol they themselves followed in grappling and contending with death.

Nurturing just the one compelling desire in the end bodes well for us—puts us in a strong position to remain focused on thoughts of the Lord alone. And as pointed out by the peerless rishis, there's this imposition taking precedence on the verge of death: On the surface of the mind stand condensed or encapsulated all of life's experiences.

The mind is the reservoir wherein the aggregate of all our past deeds, actions and thoughts are stored. And at the eleventh hour, the dying person becomes absorbed in these thoughts once again. Its the sum total *you* that shows your true colors as you take your last gasp.

While the sage takes delight in sweet reminiscences, the worldly-minded man is tormented to death. Fully commensurate on ones *karma*, the graver the sins committed, the more haunting death becomes. Its the inescapable Law of Karma that takes precedence always. Whatever a man remembers in the end was what his mind had mostly dwelt on during his lifetime. This, in turn, would determine his fate in the hereafter. According to the dictates of *karma*, our thoughts are forces of our personalities that make and remake us.

The propitious state of *nirvana* hinges on us wholly and solely being able to remember God and God alone at the time of death—the mind being completely emptied of all other thoughts. But this is well neigh impossible if we failed to master the Art of Living. And being a longwinded process, preparation has to be on an ongoing basis throughout one's life. Hence one is urged to get into the strides early.

Acting to ones own detriment and prejudices, the problem is that we are bombarded with countless amount of thoughts. Referred to as a quantum soup, scientists estimate that we entertain nearly 14,000 thoughts daily. What a mental drain and depletion of energy this is—such a stress factor to contend with especially if rooted in negativity, pessimism and ungodliness.

To negate these ill effects, one has to be in the habit of cultivating wholesome thoughts only. And in propagation thereof, everything performed by the individual from dawn to dust must be offered to the Mother of the Universe—consecrated to her cherished feet with the spirit of self-service. In utter surrender must one discharge his duties all—mentally resign himself to God.

Thus habituating ourselves, we would naturally be able to remember the Lord when matters most—when we breathe our last. And this becomes more important in the end when one has to be in constant communion with the Lord—remain fully immersed in heart, soul and consciousness with him.

With every inhalation and exhalation of breath, if one were to be so saturated in thoughts of the Lord, he shall surely get connected to the source of all life—receives the gift of Eternal Life, declared the most worshipful Lord.

THE NINTH MOMENT

Inasmuch as the last thought counts that much, it is recommended that scripture be read—or even the name of the Lord whispered into the ears of a dying person. This affords him the opportunity to bring his mind to submit solely to God—prevent any unholy thoughts seeping into his mind.

It is man's birthright to die in peace and dignity. And the sacred words of the scriptures serve as a soothing balm to his aching heart. He is thereby granted a last minute reprieve to repent and redeem himself of his sins and transgressions—a perfect time and place for confession. Like so many other things in life, the Hindus have even perfected the very *Art of Dying*. And being the chosen one, Arjuna was privy to every secret (precept) so expounded by the Cognitive Lord Sri Krishna—in divulgence whereof He entertained this wonderful conversation with him.

Arjuna
> *"How are you revealed at the hour of death*
> *to one whose consciousness is united with you?"*

Sri Krishna
> *When the time approaches for a man*
> *to leave his mortal body,*
> *he must depart with his consciousness*
> *absorbed in me and me alone.*
> *Thus he who at the time of death*
> *goes forth remembering me alone*
> *attains my abode and is united with me—*
> *comes back not to this world of mortal men.*
> *Oh Arjuna, be certain of that—*
> *have absolutely no doubt in your mind.*
> *But on the contrary,*
> *he who fails to remember me,*
> *whatever he so remembers shall be*
> *materialized unto him in the hereafter—*
> *for that was what his mind was*
> *engrossed in during his lifetime.*
> *Therefore, think of me always even*
> *in the execution of your duties.*
> *And with your mind and heart thus set upon me*
> *you will surely come to me—*
> *never must you doubt this Arjuna!*

THE SOUL EGRESS

We have already considered the soul's route of egression upon death of the average person—he who takes to the path of rebirth. But there is a procedural difference for the one who takes to the coveted path of no-return—the consummate path of *nirvana*.

Continuing to reveal to mankind the Art of Dying, Lord
Sri Krishna proclaimed to his confidant Arjuna these most
euphonious and encouraging words—secrets governing
the cryptic nature of death He withheld not:

"Thus he will take his leave:
With the life-force utterly in-drawn
and held fast between the eyebrows,
he goes forth to find his Lord,
the light-giver, the greatest!
When a man departs, he must first
close the door of his senses all.
And let him hold the mind firmly
within the shrine of his heart—
fixes the life-force between the eyebrows.
Then seeking refuge in God,
let him in steady concentration
repeat the mystic syllable Om.
And thus meditating upon God as such,
he reaches the highest goal at last!"

Getting closer to the paramount truth, Sri Krishna added
yet another dimension to what was previously mentioned.
And this has to do with the soul's egress in the case of the
Self or God-realized person—which we have just learnt is
different from that of the common man.

In the sequences followed in death, the dying person first
gathers up his senses. And they are in turn united with the
Subtle Body and Self. Then having been lit by the light of
the Self, it is by this light that the soul finally departs through
the eye or one of the other eight apertures of the body.
Here we see though the Lord repeating twice that "the life-
force finally gets affixed between the eyebrows"—

implying that it is not through the eye or some other conventional orifice of the body that the soul exits.

And now in the following section we shall learn of this important secret gateway of departure.

THE CITY OF ELEVEN GATES

There are a total of nine openings in the body. But, Yama though spoke of two others. And by way of illustration, he likened the body unto a City of Eleven Gates—conjuring up in the mind's eye the most picturesque and graphic image of the human body.

In the core of this city is found a majestic palace made out of gold—have the most imposing view of the surrounding world. And covering its fringes are eleven magnificent gates regulating the flow of traffic in and out of the royal court-yard.

Bestowed upon the chief of this city is the title of that of kingship—no other than the great potentate or ruler. And just as there was perhaps in olden days a palace in every city, so too in the body is found the citadel of the heart. And comes with it are its many decorative royal chambers—the innermost and grandest boudoir of them all being the one that houses the Self.

Nine of the eleven gates correspond to the normal bodily openings. In head alone there are seven: Two eyes, two ears, two nostrils and the mouth. Then we have the organs of reproduction and excretion. And it is through any one of these that the soul of the typical person departs.

But reserved for the seer is a special gateway of departure—a sort of red carpet treatment that awaits their blessed souls! And without further ado, Yama draws our attention to the other two openings in the body: The navel and the *sagittal suture*, a tiny fissure at the crown of the head, representing the tenth and eleventh openings respectively.

What makes the navel (umbilical cord) special is that through it one receives life. From the time of conception until birth, through it one also receives sustenance from his mother. And after it finally makes its last call, it is slammed-shut never to reopen again.

By the process of elimination then, this leaves us with the eleventh perforation only—the one so ascribed the job. Then while through the tenth opening we received the Gift of Life, through the eleventh the soul of the enlightened one majestically takes its leave.

The beauty of it all is that, whereas the tenth opening closes never to reopen again, the eleventh comes shut only to project itself open in the end if and when the need arises. Eleven all right! But how special and closely guarded are these last two.

Seen developing here is a novelty approach to death— one only the rishis have any clue or knew anything about. And much more will be said when we come to *nirvana*. But just before existing here, I shall like to end this chapter with this last thought in mind.

DEATH IS BUT A SWEET DREAM

In Hindu *eschatology* (the study of death), death is not viewed as a frightening or scary event at all. And here too the contributions made by the unmatchable, vigilant rishis must be appreciated once more. They carved out a rich and sublimed civilization for the aspiration of all mankind.

Without being obtrusive or facetious in any way, they were among the first to stipulate that death has something in common with deep dreamless sleep. And though only theoretical in nature, this hypothesis certainly looks very appealing.

In dreams, only the Gross Body is asleep—never the Subtle Body. And in examining the process leading to death, we saw that consciousness is the first thing that is affected. The senses are withdrawn into the Subtle Body, which is in no way different from what transpires during the sleeping and/or dreaming processes. But in the case of deep dreamless sleep, there is more to it.

Upon further circumspection by the rishis, it was revealed that during deep dreamless sleep not only the senses and consciousness are withdrawn, but one is also in a *desireless* state of existence. As the subtle impression of the mind vanishes, being the domain of our thoughts and feelings, the individual no longer experiences strife nor anxiety. He is said to be blissful.

The *Mandukya Upanishad* succinctly puts it this way:

"The third aspect of the Self
(referring to deep dreamless-sleep)
is the universal person called prajna.
He dreams not—he is without desire.
As the darkness of night covers the day
and the visible world seems to disappear,
so too in deepdreamless sleep the veil of unconsciousness
envelops ones being and the subtle impressions
of his mind apparently vanishes.
Seeing he no longer experiences strife or anxiety,
he is said to be blissful—the experiencer of bliss!
Having withdrawn into himself the senses and mind,
man, thus falling into a state of deep dreamless sleep,
enters the abode of the Self—is absorbed in the Self.
And as a man goes from wakefulness to dreamless sleep,

so does he too passes from life to death.
And in like manner, as a man goes from
deep dreamless sleep to wakefulness
so does he too, at the time of death,
passes from this life to the next!'

During deep dreamless sleep, our consciousness is withdrawn from the physical body, Subtle Body and mind as well. The mind lies completely still as we rest in the lap of the Self. Absorbed in the Self, we become oblivious to whom or what we are. But upon awakening, we assume our same old personalities all over again.

The rishis certainly makes death look easy on us. They were of the general unanimity and belief that it is not such a big deal after all. As pointed out here, all there is to it is simply passing back-and-forth—falling asleep and waking up again. Deep dreamless sleep is the veil which those who live call life—those who don't death.

Every night we go to sleep we literally pass out—only to be sprung back into action when awakened in the morning. How is death and rebirth any different—daily doses of which are administered unto us.

Death seems an oddity only because of our obtuse minds. The rishis somehow correctly saw death as a welcome guest. It is not as obfuscated as it is made out to be. They took the sting and stigma out of it. It's nothing but a sweet dream—a sound, deep dreamless-sleep. So that you may extract the true esoteric meaning hereof, I strongly recommend that you read and reread this section carefully. And as you do, try to fathom the depths of the rishis minds.

POINT OF SPECIAL INTEREST

Trying not to divert your attention much, here's something

ancillary I want to share with you. Even though the subtle impression of the mind vanishes during deep dreamless sleep (man enters a state of oblivion), the subconscious mind still harbors desires, hopes and aspirations.

And seeing that the same holds true for death, it implies then that the more we are attached to material things, the more painful death becomes—more difficult it is to have our consciousness wrenched away. And this is exactly why the rishis strongly advocate us getting rid of all unwanted desires. They assured us that it will offset the rigormortis that comes with death.

Prior to death, a yogi does not experience the same pain as is evident in the life of the average man. As far as he is concerned, there's complete annihilation of desires. And ever so much his peaceful and tranquil self, he stands tall in whatever situation he finds himself in—enact fully the stately principles of equanimity.

❈ *Thirteen* ❈

Nirvana

THE STATE OF UNION WITH BRAHMAN

THE desideratum and quintessence of life, *nirvana* is contingent upon extinction and immolation of all desires—to divest oneself of them all totally. It is the redemptive state whereby all karmic debts are fully repaid. And whereupon also, the individual is freed from their mandates thereof—engendering in finality precipitation and union with the Supreme Spirit.

Upon examination of the key elements and components of this definition, much was already said about desires and *karma*. Therefore it's the latter part of the definition we would be concerned here with: The process of synthesis espoused by the ebullient and pertinacious rishis whereby man could defeat death—merges his identity with the One Absolute.

Considering the intricacies and implied nature typified of this form of discussion, I shall reintroduce a simile made before that becomes even more meaningful here in the end, which, under no circumstances, should fall on deaf ears—be like casting pearls before swine.

CONQUERING DEATH

It's like at birth you are given a piece of diamond that upon the end of life's journey you are required to return to the Giver. Mistaken it as being fake, some of us may return it in the same manner given to us. Some in a worst state, while others, much to the satisfaction of the Lord, may return it as a solitaire piece of jewelry.

The tragedy or irony is that by innocently toying with it, getting it tarnished, and having it returned in a defiled manner, what could you come to expect from the Giver. And analogically speaking, this precious gem could undoubtedly be likened unto the soul of man.

Conquering death means being in a position whereby we surrender this gift in its original pristine form and glory. And having reached this state of immaculate perfection, one is fit and ready to take the final plunge in uniting oneself with the Lord of unsullied purity—man surrendering his precious soul to God as he would the diamond alluded to above.

When we were born we were of a clear conscience. We came into this world with clean hands—hearts made out of gold. And when we cease to be we must return intact—an expectation not unwarranted (or unreasonable) by any means.

Presented below is a wonderful comparison I would like you to consider. Realizing that *nirvana* involves merging our individual souls with that of Gods, let's examine what takes place at the beginning of life (at the time of conception) to see if it has anything in common with what takes place at the end (at the time of death).

PROCESS IN COMMON

Attempting now to get it down to a science, it reminds me what was taught us in Cytology (a branch of advanced biology devoted to the study of the structure, function and life history of cells). Here in the laboratory we were able to view under the microscope exactly how cells come together, fuse, and eventually become one.

And being also evident in human reproduction, we would now determine whether or not any parallel could be drawn here at all. We want to see if there are any similarities between what takes place when we enter our mothers' wombs as opposed to the cosmic womb, nay, not the bowels of the earth as some may want to term it.

Throughout the centuries mankind has been groping in darkness where the miraculous development of life in the womb was concerned. Shedding light to this mystery, speculation turned into reality when it was proven that two specialized germ cells or gametes (the female *ovum* and the male *spermatozoon*) fuse in order to give rise to the first cell of the *embryo* or *zygote*.

Prior to fusion, however, the ovum and spermatozoon must first be prepared in a special way by a process known as *meiosis*—whereby the 46 chromosomes of each cell are reduced by half (to 23). This process is necessary in that when the two cells eventually come together, they will yield the full composite 46 chromosomes.

As it approaches the ovum, the cap on the head of the spermatozoon dissolves, enabling it to penetrate through the wall of the ovum. And as soon as the first spermatozoon enters, the electrical charge on the ovum membrane gets altered, making it virtually impassable to all the other germ cells.

Once inside the ovum, the head of the spermatozoon swells and breaks loose its encoded genetic information. And no sooner said than done, they cleave together giving rise to what's now referred to as the "fertilized ovum"— the DNA blueprint necessary to commence development of the human embryo.

What a process to speak about! Labeling it the *Labor of Love*, this is how I would like to dramatize this truly remarkable incidence:

> *Two cells made half,*
> *and from opposite sexes too,*
> *coming together in progeny*
> *for the sheer joy of life —*
> *verily a gift from God*
> *through the nobility of parenthood!*

Call it whatever you like, this eventful beginning of life in the womb is the wonder of all wonders! These reproductive cells are endowed with such a remarkable degree of intelligence and potentiality that even after coming together the rest of the process takes place on its own accord.

And if it's true at the cellular level, then why not also at the human level—and for that matter the cosmic level too. Inasmuch as it happens at the beginning of life, why not also at the end—a process whereby two entities eventually become one? And in the case of birth it's two cells, whereas at death two souls—the micro and the macro souls.

Nature operates with such precision and meticulousness that once the contact is made or the process initiated, the rest of it takes place spontaneously. And apart from reproduction in the zoological kingdom, we see the same happening too in botanical world—exemplified by *pollination* and *grafting*.

Metamorphosis of a butterfly is yet another striking phenomena occurring in nature that is a marvel to behold—such drastic transformation taking place right before our naked eyes: It starts with the egg that hatches into a worm-like caterpillar, followed by the appalled looking larva that finally gives rise to a markedly colorful butterfly.

Having witnessed changes such as these occurring in nature, what's all this dubiousness when comes time to accept the "human metamorphosis." Albeit in a spiritual sense, man too metamorphosed as he undergoes the many stupendous evolutionary changes, culminating ultimately in the wondrous state of *nirvana*.

MEANS TO AN END

Having looked at this remarkable parallelism, let's now get down to the heart of the matter. And with a discussion on prayer also pending, I shall now endeavor to show you why *nirvana* is principally achieved only through the medium of meditation—the main vehicle to get us there.

Thus it becomes imperative for us to have a good grounding on both of these important techniques. And trying to be as cogent as possible, I would have to swerve and go a bit off tangent here—take you slightly off course to demonstrate how cogitable a proposition prayer and meditation is.

But so that we do not loose track of where we're heading, I shall bring you back in a hurry. And then we would explore how one gets connected to God, applying of course the puissant techniques of these two remarkable guiding principles.

But first I want to address two other pertinent subject matters before so doing: Right Mindset and Man's Final Resolve.

RIGHT MINDSET

Including *nirvana*, nothing is impossible to achieve in this world if one has the proper mindset. Reaching and becoming one with God means harboring the desire to do so—

plant the seed of *Right Intention*. And this in turn becomes the catalyst to activate the process.

Registering this intention with the brain and sub-conscious mind is the sure first step needed taken. The intention here is to feel God's overwhelming presence—wanting to get connected to him. Pointing the mind towards God sets the soul on an automatic course.

How would you expect the fruit if you've never planted the seed? And after planting it, wouldn't it be sometime before it geminates, grows and bears fruit? Intention is the seed that lies at the heart of the process.

Using another analogy, how would you possibly get to Paris if you've not first contemplated the idea of so doing? And wouldnt it be the same if you want to go back to where you belong—your place of origin and home sweet home? The sooner you entertain the idea the quicker you'll be en-route to your place of destination—back to the Godhead whom you seek to be with.

Hence one must be careful what his wishes and aspirations are for they may very likely come true. No wonder then pessimistic individuals find bad things happening to them all the time. And suffice to say, anything can be achieved by invoking the boundless spirit in man.

There's a divine light in each and every one of us. Albeit a minuscule one in the mediocre person, it is greatly magnified in the holy and pure at heart. And once lit, it glows brighter and brighter until the whole of ones personality becomes fully illumined.

Like an entrepreneur would first sit down and prepare his Business Plans, similarly mapping out ones spiritual strategies makes good sense. Think of it! If you're to give up a fraction of your life daily to God, wouldn't you soon become the most enlightened person there is?

Apart from the magic of writing it down, this is the power of knowing what you want and having a Plan of Action to achieve it. And seeing that time is always of the essence, it is what it takes also to unwind the soul—a process once initiated follows its own natural, biological rhythmic-pattern.

FINAL RESOLVE

And speaking about *mindset, nirvana* is by far the most important resolve in one's life. The goal of all goals, *nirvana* must be made to captivate our full attention—garner all of our physical and mental energies in the championing of this cause. And here's one instance where the means would always justify the end.

Forging right ahead, man just prior to this propitious moment must maintain constant vigilance and communion with God. And being that it could only be materialized through the application of meditation and prayer, these two important tools are considered the most intriguing examples where reaching and making contact beyond material reality is concerned.

THE POWER OF PRAYER

"If you know how to give good gifts to your children
how much more wouldn't the Father in heaven
give Holy Spirit to those of his children who ask of him!"
—*The Holy Bible*

Prayer is man's liturgical formulation to God—his humble supplications, entreaties and praises to the Monotheistic and Venerable Father in heaven. And considered the soul's yearning or clamoring for the divine, man can no easier befriend or win the Divine Grace.

In our belief of a Higher or Supernatural Power, it is via the satellite-like effects of prayer that we can orbit (surf) God's world—complete the circuit of God's divine flow of energy. We become receptive to signals emitted afar, picked up here on earth on account of the ingenuity of the human species.

But apart from maintaining communion with God, prayer is also paying homage and adoration to Him. With bended knees, man, in the process of so doxologizing and propitiating the Lord, could inevitably invoke His sweet benign blessings—prayerfully lifts his heart up to Him in deep reverence and devotion.

Prayer placates and appeases the mind—keeps it virtually intact. And with constant practice and application, it even purifies our thoughts and actions. It takes us closer and closer to God—secures for us a place in his Holy Kingdom or Being.

Being the most conventional or orthodox way to contact God, we find that when we pray we actually receive God's amazing grace—get what we want. And just as stated in the *Holy Bible*: "Ask and it shall be given. Knot and it shall be opened unto you. Seek and ye shall find"— no idle or meek promises made unto man by God.

In short then, prayer is the medium to invoke and reach out to God—an initiative that rests squarely on our shoulders. And our blessed founding fathers who first sat down to write our constitution were certainly of the right presence of mind. Leaving no stones unturned, they saw to it fit to have the Freedom of Worship securely preserved— an inscription that found its way unto the very parchment on which our Charter of Rights and Freedoms were first scrolled.

And with jurisprudence in mind, here's a comparison you would find very interesting. As a deponent or defendant in Court is under oath to tell the truth, so too prayer is like standing before a judge—albeit the most important of all judges.

Getting ready to make your final submissions, you would walk up to the podium and respectfully begin to speak—hoping to win every little favor with the judge. And the very first thing you would do is bow and acknowledge his over-whelming presence—your first words being: "Your honor!"

And right after so doing you would cease the slightest opportunity that presents itself to praise him. And in reci-tation of the Lord's Prayer we do just the same, as we bow our heads in prayer: "Our Father who art in heaven, hal-lowed be thy name. Thy kingdom come."

Then making yourself as electrifying and charming as you possibly could, you would politely ask the judge what it is you are seeking—an approach well portrayed and ex-emplified also in the Lord's Prayer: "Give us this day our daily bread."

And if you are guilty of any wrongdoing, you would be ill advised not to quickly get on your knees and ask for for-giveness—demonstrate to the judge how remorseful and repentant you are. And the same goes too for the Lords Prayer: "Forgive our debts, those who have trespassed against us, as we forgive our debtors.

As you appropriately began your submissions with ac-knowledgment and praises, so too must you end it. And for this reason, an experience attorney may even want to preface his closing remarks with words of commendation: "Your Honor, in the name of Her Majesty the Queen, there is hardly any instance of a miscarriage of justice in this great land of ours"

And the same holds true too where the Lord Prayer is concerned, which also ends on this very same high, distinc-tive note: "For thine is the Kingdom, and the power, and the glory, forever and ever. Amen."

As in judicial submissions, God is not interested in the nitty-gritty of the matter. Having already heard it all in the often boring and protracted trial, the judge seems to be saying now: "Let thy words be but few—speak tersely and with brevity. Please get to the bone of the contention."

And as the whole of law is premised on finding the intent or motive behind ones actions, so too God wants to know where lie our hearts! And supposedly being of a contrite one, one must in all earnestness repent and atone for his mistakes. Speak your heart out to Him for God is the most understanding of them all.

SCIENTIFIC RATIONALE FOR PRAYER

By just thinking of the Lord as we do in prayers, it produces subtle waves of vibrations the Prescient Father becomes immediately receptive to. And you can vouchsafe he would also be made responsive to. Coming under the influence of God's Holy Spirit, its such a purposeful force to reckon with.

From a purely applied and scientific approach then, prayer is much more stereotyped and efficacious than one would like to believe. It is viewed as the journey into consciousness beyond all ordinary thought processes—a transcending process that defies every logic in the book.

It is seen as registering ones intention deep down beyond space-time boundary. Sounding more like a quantum phenomenon, it implicates the brain and the whole of ones being in this cooperative enterprise with God—the establishing of a sweet intimacy between the individual and Supreme Spirits.

Just the other day I came across a report showing that churchgoers suffer less stress and live longer. And many other such studies were done that would attest to the values and benefits derived from prayers. When all else fails, man's last resort is to prostrate himself before God in prayer.

Trying to estimate the power and promise prayer holds, here's a couple of other studies that would demonstrate just that. Again Chopra in his book *How to Know God* wrote:

"Beginning more than twenty years ago researchers devised experiments in an attempt to verify whether or not prayer has any effect at all on some seriously ill patients. These patients were divided into two groups: Ones being prayed-for, and ones not. And to everyone's astonishment the breaking news was that the ones prayed-for recovered better, regardless whether or not they knew the persons doing the prayer or were even so informed.

Again in 1998 a Duke University team proved to the utter amazement of all skeptics that prayer indeed has certain efficacy. Taking into account all manner of variables (including heart rate and blood pressure) researchers took 150 patients who underwent invasive cardiac procedures and requested several groups of people around the globe to pray for them.

Seven such religious groups offered prayers, including Buddhists in Nepal and Carmelite nuns in Baltimore and Virtual Jerusalem. And at the end of it all it was shown that these surgical patients recovery was 50 to 100 percent better if someone had only prayed for them—again whether or not it was known to the patients what was happening."

Call it whatever you like, prayer works. And if done with implicit faith it can even move mountains—work wonders in your life. And looking at the full dimension and scope of it, it can be concluded that many things are wrought by prayer than the world dreams of.

And there could be no better time and place to solicit and petition the gracious Lord's help. In the nick of time (at the time of death), man should pray open his heart and recite reward-orientated prayers such as the ones mentioned below—be it even though a modicum or shred of it so offered.

Thus impregnated and full of faith, the mind is thereby brought under arrest and made to submit solely to Brahman; for it is only with the help of Brahman one can be united with Brahman. And being also a symbol of Brahman, Agni the god of fire is also hereby propitiated.

EXAMPLES OF PRAYERS

May quietness descend upon
my limbs, speech, breath, eyes, ears.
May all my senses wax clear and strong.
May Brahman show himself unto me now.
Never must I deny Brahman
nor Brahman deny me.
I'm with him, and he's with me.
May we abide always together.
May Brahman be revealed unto me—
the one who is devoted to him always!

*　　*　　*

Oh god Agni lead me to felicity.
Thou knowest all my deeds.
Preserve me from the deceitful attractions of sin.
To thee I offer my salutation, again and yet again!

*　　*　　*

Let my life now merge
into the All-pervading life.

> *Ashes are my body's end.*
> *Oh mind, remember Brahman.*
> *Oh mind, remember thy past deeds.*
> *Remember Brahman.*
> *Remember thy past deeds.*

Then this native American prayer:

> *"Make me always ready to come to you*
> *with clean hands and straight eyes,*
> *so that when life fades away*
> *like the dwindling daylight,*
> *my spirit may come to you without shame."*

In the foregoing verses we earnestly request that may we never deny Brahman nor Brahman deny us. May we always abide with each other. And being our birthright, precious legacy and story of our glorious human heritage, we conjure and beseech the Lord that may we be identi-fied with him in the end.

But if perchance we fail to achieve this milestone, we pray that may our good deeds (*karma*) accompany us— dictate for us a quality life in our next birth. May we be blessed with the next best option—rebirth as a pious and virtuous soul.

PERTINENT QUESTIONS

Having considered the potency of prayer, we would now turn our attention over to meditation. And as a preamble to our discussions let's look at the *Swetasvatara Upanishad* where some of the most crucial advices were given—in elucidation whereof we are presented with this very fascinating and exegetical communiqué:

> *"He who is beyond cause and effect*
> *must be meditated upon in order to*

transcend physical consciousness.
The seers so absorbed in meditation
saw within themselves the ultimate reality—
the Self-luminous Brahman that dwells
as the conscious entity in all creatures.
Thus with the aid of meditation
you will realize the Self as being
separate from the body.
And thus he shall surely reach union
with the Lord of immortality—
become identified with him.
The truth is that you were always
united with the God of love
but just that you don't know that.
And in the words of the Lord:
"From me all emerge.
In me all exist.
To me all shall return.
I am Brahman—
One without a second!"

Nothing is further from the truth! And the truth is that unbeknown to us, we've always been united with the God of love, but just that we are not conscious of it. And coming to the realization that the Self is an adjunct of Brahman, all fetters are loosened and ignorance vanished—man no longer being affected by diseases, old age, and death.

Thus we could transcend the plane of physical consciousness and reach union with the Lord of Immortality through the power of prayer and meditation. And repeatedly we are hearing the word meditation being mentioned. In fact it is what it all boils down to in the end.

And referring back to our previous discussions on *turiya*, references were already made to the fourth state. It is the supreme abode of the immortal Self reachable only by the virtue of meditation. And for this very same reason also even *nirvana* is made incidental to meditation.

It's the one and only vehicle there is to accomplish this difficult end. It will get us across the boundary that separates us from the Self.

BORDER CROSSING

When death is nigh, one needs to implement the power of the will in order to curtail the senses and mind—have them moved into the undifferentiated consciousness mode. And here again meditation comes to man's rescue. It's the only known impetus that could actuate the process to get and keep us in life eternal.

Just as there are waves and turbulence on the surface of an ocean but deep down its waters are held in silence, similarly he who lives on the surface of his existence experiences the storm of life—comes into contact with the blizzard, squall and commotion it variegates!

And in stark contrast thereto, life is more sublime and peaceful for the one whose consciousness runs deep—he who discovers the haven of peace and quietude that's already there. And this is attainable only by delving deep down the bottom of ones existence through the mechanization and strength of meditation.

Found hidden in the heart, the rishis saw that the Self is held in occlusion or at bay from the rest of the world—separated and ensconced as if by an imaginary boundary. And nothing invasively or otherwise easily gets across this barricade. All evils shun the Self for deep within lies it shielded from all impediments.

Let's now look at how the Upanishads portray this boundary. And having done so we shall make a minor detour or two before coming head-on with the crossing of it—which again is accomplished only by the initiative of meditation.

> *"Like being protected by a boundary,*
> *the Self within the lotus of the heart*
> *is divided from the rest of the world.*
> *Day and night do not cross that boundary*
> *and neither also are good nor evil deeds,*
> *grief nor pleasure, old age nor death.*
> *All evils shun the Self for deep within*
> *lies the Self shielded from all afflictions—*
> *untouched and free of all impurities.*
> *He who crosses this boundary,*
> *if he is blind, wounded or aggrieved*
> *is no longer so affected.*
> *And being that Brahman is light itself,*
> *by crossing this boundary night becomes day!"*

Diving into this pure unitary and undifferentiated field of consciousness requires not just a mere trip per se. And although it is an almost insurmountable task to unlock the door of the imperial chamber wherein lies the soul royally enthroned, it is made possible only through the virtue of meditation—achieving which all the complexities of life are completely obliterated.

HIGHEST RECOMPENSE

Although a gregarious animal, man has to walk life in a single file in the end. And in compliance thereof, the sages highest recompense is to become solely entrenched in God so that after death they may never again have to return to the woeful status of mortal men—to this world of imperfection.

Cognizance of the fact that the Self resides within the lotus of their hearts, they daily meditated and entered that holy sanctuary consecrated to the Self. And having drank of that nectar, the indefatigable Sage becomes inebriated with divine ecstasy—frees himself from identity with his body.

This climax is reached only when one crosses this boundary and gets quite beyond, affording man the rare opportunity to link himself with the Supreme Reality. Like the smooth and continuous flow of oil poured from one container into another, so also must ones consciousness be made to flow in an unbroken stream.

By wholly and solely meditating upon the Self, one avails himself the most powerful weapon in his hands. As laser is a potent beam of light, in like manner intense mediation can be made to possess laser-like sharpness. As a lamp flickers not in a windless place, so too can one unflinchingly penetrate to the core of his being with the aid of meditation.

For this reason too the wisest of gurus even prescribe a holy *mantram* to be used in conjunction with meditation. The mere repetition of it can be made sharp as a sword to cut through the veil of *maya* (delusion). And by thus holding the mind one-pointedly focused, it produces the resultant effect a torch may have on impregnable steel—penetrates its object like a well guided missile.

Chopra reminds us that as "the mantra grows fainter and fainter, it eventually fades away. And at that point, one's awareness crosses the quantum boundary. Consequently, the material plane is left behind and we find ourselves in a region where spiritual activities command its own laws."

With the powers of the mind thus harnessed and channeled, one is now positioned to realize his sole goal—

the crowning peace *nirvana*. And as such, man can consider himself having achieved the primary or fundamental objective of his life.

Having now learnt how to contact the Self, the next step is finding or locating God. And once that is accomplished we shall then have to figure out just how the rishis effectuated this union of souls—theirs with that of God's. Its an achievement that has made them the envy of world.

But before that, let's see how the assertions made pertaining to this boundary tie-in with scientific models proposed by the contemporary genius Deepak Chopra! And his work I am referring to has to do with the division of reality into the Material, Quantum and Virtual Domains.

An ardent lover or admirer of the rishis himself, perhaps Chopra too got his inspirations right here from these very infectious words of theirs—whereby stemmed too these brilliant deductions of his. And for our comprehension, Chopra quantified and expressed it all in familiar scientific terms.

LOCATING GOD'S DOMAIN

Becoming privy to the whereabouts of someone makes it easier to locate that person—failing which, it would be like looking for a needle in a haystack. And trying to pinpoint the locality of God, Chopra's premise makes good sense once again—which should come to us as no surprise at all.

Creating a new perspective, model, and approach, he brilliantly envisages *reality* falling under three categories— a sort of three-dimensional stratification of the universe if you will. And this in itself has led to many startling possibilities—opened up a whole new dimension for us. And they are:

Material Domain: It corresponds to the material plane

we see and behold right before our eyes—this physical world we have come to know and live in.

Quantum Domain: Found lying just above the Material is the Quantum Domain—the transitional zone to God where the soul begins.

Virtual Domain: Superior to the other two is the Virtual Domain of God—the place beyond time and space that represents the very origin of the universe.

Getting back to our concerns of being able to cross this boundary, we now see clearly what the rishis were alluding to before. And very cleverly, Chopra has qualitatively and quantitatively identified it for us—this boundary claimed by the rishis to be so intriguing.

Whereas the body lies exclusively at the Material Domain, the Self is held in occlusion deep down at the Quantum level—a place that is beyond the plane of material consciousness. But even quite further beyond lies the Virtual Domain where God resides, separated as He is from the soul of man and the physical body.

For the sake of clarity, it can be hypothetically explained as a threefold transcending process. There is this need to go the distance—travel from the Material, to the Quantum, to the Virtual Domain. And this is what our main focus would be here.

Doesn't one get stuck all his life at the Material Domain—think of himself as a mere physical being and no more. But what he is really is a god in the making! Just that he needs to take steps to cash in on his good fortune. And here is his chance of doing just that.

DOMAIN DOMINANCE

It is a verifiable and well-known fact of life! Everything at the Material Domain is subject to birth, death and decay.

And falling into this deathtrap, man does not bother to look beyond, which, if he were to, he would find a place where nothing is ever born, grows old nor dies. And this place is known as the Quantum Realm.

And there are very good reasons behind this too. Scientists have explained that the Quantum Domain does not have to obey any of the physical laws operative here in the material plane. It's a whole new ball game altogether—a supernatural world all by itself.

Doomed as he is in thinking of himself as the material body only, man is led to believe that he shall one day die—his existence forever terminated. And being that the body exists at this level, it is not difficult to see why he thinks, acts and behaves that way.

How erroneous and pathetic it is for man to pin his trust solely on material reality only—try to decipher everything using it as the only yardstick! It's about time we loosen our grip and travel beyond the primary and secondary level to the all-important tertiary level—the level where dwells God. And if we were to, we would notice a huge difference in our lives.

THE INTRICATE INTER-RELATIONSHIP

Referred to as the *river of life,* Chopra proposes that the flow of all biological impulses go from the Virtual, to the Quantum, to the Material Plane. This means then that our thoughts do in fact have divine origins—come from the Virtual or God-Force-Field, and not the other way around.

Then filtering their way through the Quantum Zone, they finally surface here in the material hemisphere. And this reminds me of the unforgettable words of Yama that finds fulfillment here: "When all is well, the Self makes all decisions." And though recorded several thousand years ago, how meaningful it is even in this day and age of Quantum Physics.

As a quantum creature, man is advantageously positioned. Being that the Quantum Domain is the place where the soul begins, it is more or less the transitional zone or doorway to God. It acts very much like a carrier that vacillates back-and-forth the Quantum and Virtual Domains.

And in a moment you would see that when comes time to do so, the soul would eventually travel beyond the Quantum Zone—link us with God in his Virtual Rendezvous or Cosmic Hiding Place.

LINKAGE WITH GOD

"That Paramatma (Universal Soul) is perfect.
That Atman (individual soul) is perfect.
Perfect is born from perfect.
Take away perfect from perfect
and what remains is also perfect!"
—The Upanishads

When asked by Arjuna, the blessed Lord Sri Krishna defined the soul as being *jivatman*. And dissecting or taking this word apart, Chopra makes a very subtle but important distinction—one that drives home the true meaning of the much sophisticated human soul.

Broken down into two syllables, *jiva* corresponds to the individual soul making its long journey throughout many births. It is what is involved in *karma*—whereupon all seeds of karmic actions are imputed and stored. In short, it's that part of the soul that gives rise to our unique, distinctive human traits—a blue print of our true physical identity.

And *Atman* on the other hand represents Brahman or

the part God in man—the ever so pure, uncontaminated portion of it. And irrespective of how good or bad an individual may be, the *Atman* is never in any way affected. It is a constant—the quality common in everyone be it the worst of criminals or the holiest of saints.

Then whereas jiva preserves our individuality, *Atman* takes on the role of becoming universal—consummated in the end when it finally unites with God. And I urge you to make a mental note of this very important point—one that can in no way be overemphasized.

Being then part human (*jiva*) and part God (*Atman*), the soul is seen as possessing a dual nature or disposition. Enjoying "VIP" status, the *Atman* doesn't have to travel to reach God. It never left in the first place, being itself fixedly aligned with God always.

And whereas *jiva* lives at the quantum level, *Atman* is found inveterately anchored deep down at the Virtual Level. It's like having one foot in the Quantum Domain while maintaining our firm stance with God in his Virtual Domain—man and God moving in tandem with each other.

THE GOLDEN HANDSHAKE

And this is what *nirvana* is precisely all about: How one in affiance thereto effectively gets connected to God. And from hereon now there would be a total shift in perspective—a more concerted and conscientious effort made in effecting it.

And to begin with, we find that in addition to the *threefold* division mentioned above, Chopra extrapolated another model for us to consider. He showed the Quantum Zone as being the passageway or viaduct leading to the higher sphere where Good is.

Here the picture gets even much clearer: God (who is

within sight) can be reached only if we care to meet him halfway—trancend this fine line of demarcation. And this implies then that God and humans have this confluence or common meeting ground.

As discussed before, we normally have glimpses of God's World by such phenomena such as Visions, Miracles, Telepathy, ESP, Clairvoyance, Synchronicity. Serving to bridge the two worlds for us, man has this gravitational or magnetic pull going for him.

Applying a twist or trajectory to it, Chopra proposes yet another model. As if God is in a world all by Himself, he drew this circle in which only God is found. And at the edge or periphery of the circle is the soul, knocking at the door of God.

What is even more interesting is that he showed the mind following immediately behind—the driving force of the soul in its charge to penetrate this barrier. And getting closer to the paramount truth, we could see that the mind plays the key role here—becomes intimately involved in the whole process.

As would see, it is the one charged with the responsibility of executing this most difficult task at hand—effecting this coalition between the micro and macro souls through the aid of meditation.

GETTING ONLINE WITH GOD

Before we consider how one actually gets online with God, I will divert a little and show you how the All-knowing Father would want to prepare us for this most eventful meeting—this face-to-face encounter with God. And tying it all together, Sri Krishna made this startling validation— how the expectant man must conduct himself at this most crucial juncture:

"Make it a habit to practice meditation,
and do not let your mind be distracted.
In this way you will finally come to me.
On me let him meditate,
for at the final trumpet sound,
he shall be saved by the strength
of this yoga faithfully followed.
With a serene and fearless heart,
let him struggle to reach my oneness—
hold the mind from its restless roaming,
ever absorbed in mind, body and soul on me.
Then seeking refuge in me,
let him, in steady meditation,
repeat the mystic syllable Om.
Thus, having control over the mind,
and meditating upon the Lord as such,
one shall at last be bestowed
the crowning peace of nirvana—
the peace that is in me.
As a lamp flickers not in a windless place,
so too must you one-pointedly fix your mind
upon the Atman—think of it and nothing else.
And no matter where the restless mind wanders,
it must be drawn back and made to submit to it."

The Lord repeatedly referred to the mind. And here we would see what a pivotal role it plays. And this should come to us as no surprise at all especially when so much emphasis was already placed on mind control. You would remember how Lord Krishna cautioned us not to underestimate nor devalue the benefits accruing thereto.

Aided and abetted by the intransient senses, the mind could easily cut us a raw deal—have our lives ransacked and ravaged. Therefore, steps must be taken early to bring the vagrant senses under the superintendence of the mind—be made subservient and obedient to it.

If grounded and brought under servitude of the mind, the senses could, in this case, prove itself indispensably necessary in man's stride for liberation—display the much needed esprit de corps (loyalty) when it matters most.

But apart from the helpful mind, initiation and forging of this linkage or fraternity with the Divine has a lot to do with other biological changes simultaneously taking place. It involves the brain and mind coming into play with the soul and God in this supreme cause of action.

Chopra's rationality hinges on the fact that, inasmuch as radio is the receiver of sound signals, similarly the brain is the receiver of the mind. As a matter-of-fact, the brain is our only available means of registering reality—spirit being filtered through biology, he wrote.

The brain is what enables us to move from simple survival instincts to God consciousness. It helps to lift man from the thresholds of his much retrogressive animalistic propensities to godliness. How infinite in resources are our much evolved nervous system—more particularly so the brain.

But, though the brain is hardwired to find God, it is not an automatic process. You must have in place the proper mindset and desire. And then given proper application (constantly engaging oneself in TM) the brain progressively gets coherent or congruent—becomes impregnated with such remarkable spiritual superfluity.

And becoming more and more intensified with the passage of time, it eventually leads to a fulsome state of mental satiety. It takes man to the point where he becomes fully enamored and overwhelmed. It, inasmuch, results in an irresistible attraction or bonding of some sort. And with whom else can it be but God who is drawing nigh?

Picking up on these euphoric and sensational cerebral outbursts, man enters a state of profound and heightened awareness. And this state of spiritual inebriety undeniably comes about only by employing and engaging oneself in undeviated meditation on the *Atman* and God.

Elaborating on the power of meditation, Maharshi Mahesh Yogi puts it this way. 'With practice, the nervous system becomes habituated not to lose that heightened state of awareness...and that state is now being maintained during waking, dreaming and sleeping. Therefore, beginning to take over here is a form of supra-consciousness— starting with the higher centers of one's awareness that can intuit God presence and moving down to ever pore of one's body.'

MAKING THE ACTUAL CONNECTION

Courted and wooed by the mind, the compliant, tamed and rehabilitative senses can be made obsequious and subordinate to the mind. And this consequentially enables the mind to act more like a radar, preventing us going astray from our contemplated path—the *no-return* destination seeks man.

Being contiguously placed within close proximity to the soul, the mind, in propinquity thereto, slowly gravitates and encroaches on the soul. And following the line of lease resistance, the soul, at the final trumpet sound, concomitantly crosses over to God's Domain—resulting in the interstitial relationship between the individual and cosmic soul about to acquiesce, cohere and harmonize.

And in consignment thereof, man in full cry tenders his soul over to God—the individual soul concatenates or lapses into the Being of all Beings. And being of the same wavelength, it is understandable why they readily accept each other—hit this happy medium.

Hence, the soul precipitously gets superimposed in the most splendiferous manner—man and God having been meant for each other. And if I am to state this any differently, it would be to say that: Being of such autochthonous, cognate and close kinship, the micro and macro souls are left with no further alternative but to coalesce, fuse and become one.

In fructification thereof, man and his benignant Soulmate (God) renew their fraternal bond. Arm-in-arm, the soul is embryonically engulfed, embraced and cuddled by the Mother of the Universe—the Fairy Godmother really. It is extended this unparalleled comity or cordiality now that man finds himself on the lap of the most affectionate Father.

Given their presumed kindred and consanguineous relationship (like raindrops longing to return to the seas), the individual symbiocally gets naturalized to his fully blossomed or fulsome state. He rightfully enters his long awaited erstwhile relationship with God—a camaraderie that candidly leaves nothing else to be desired.

THE DEDUCTION

Demonstrated in the fusion and cleavage of the ovum and spermatozoon, it is the same process being advocated here also—a consubstantiality that is in no way different. And seeing there's so much of the right chemistry, affinity and compatibility already existing between them, coming together again like forces of opposing magnets is made relatively easy.

As you would remember, once this contact is made between the ovum and spermatozoon, the rest of the process takes place spontaneously. Nature finds a way to carry out, effectuate or consummate the alliance.

Crossing from the Quantum to the Virtual Domain, space and time collapse. And being the place where all things are cradled and ultimately laid to rest also, the Virtual Domain is said to be the *Port of Permanent Call*—man being stately laid to rest in the person of the Affable Protectorate.

The soul finally escheats to its indigenous sacrarium—summarily goes back to the place where it began as a soul. Call it the place where it both commences and also convenes, the *genesis* as well as the *final siesta* for the good and pious souls.

Nirvana then represents, closing of the last minuscule gap (the identify-and-difference) between man and God—a stage whereby that infinitesimal point is now expanded into infinitude. And having thus been consecrated back to the Creator, the individual becomes the god he seeks to be all his life—man in his flight to true stardom.

And without any further rhetoric nor having to be condescending in any way, the resultant effect is that there is now no apparent difference between you and God. In unity all separation ends. By merging, the souls become one—totally inseparable thereafter.

It's like the rivers! Having reached and entered the ocean, man no longer speaks of the rivers. They see only of the ocean. Similarly, having sunk ones soul or identity in God, everyone thereafter speaks only of God.

In this holy betrothal or wedlock, man bears the semblance or impersonation of the Holy Father Himself. Like father, like son! There's this familiarity, oneness, closeness redeveloping between him—flesh of his flesh, bones of his bones, soul of his soul.

Spiritual evolution is now complete. Man finds his place in the Eternal Flow—in the God whom he reveres all of his life. It's the vindication of life's sole purpose brought to fruition and fecundity—a hypothesis that makes death a laughable impossibility.

THE ART OF DYING

I shall now attempt to bring you this recapitulation. Having precognition of his impending fate, the provost seer who rules over his senses and mind, would, at this penultimate stage, preferably sit in the yogic lotus posture—legs folded and spine erect if possible.

And instead of falling into a pensive mood, he probes himself into an elated and exuberant frame of mind fully engrossed in wrapped meditation or *samadhi*—the highest form of imageless trance with the formless Brahman.

Well disposition and in bated breath too, the postulant seeker now takes this final and most crucial plunge of all. Fully predicated on the strength of meditation, death for the illumined Yogi is predestined as follows:

- Having mortified the flesh and subdued the senses, the first or precursory step is to bring the mind under the firmest of control.
- Moved into this cryptic mode, the individual with stoic patience and forbearance gathers up his senses about him.
- And after completely withdrawing their powers (they are made non-functional) his body is wholly and solely rendered unconscious.
- Gathering up next *prana* (the vital energy), the senses and *prana* become united with the Subtle Body (comprising of the mind, intellect and ego) which in turn is mounted by the Self.
- The senses, *prana*, Subtle Body and the Self (referred collectively to as the *vital life-force)* conjoin as a unit.

And in this conjunctive state, they together descend into the heart at the point where the nerves join.

- Lit by the light of the Self, it is by this light that the *vital life-force* is now positioned to take its leave of the body.
- Drawn up next through the *Sushumna* or Central Spinal Passage the soul, in this betokened and portentous state gets betwixt the eyebrows.
- All along engaged in unswerving meditation while repeating the sacred password *Om*, the individual is ready to take refuge in the Lord. Thus remembering God, the Yogi is said to be absorbed in consciousness with him.
- Then, at this most opportune and felicitous moment, he royally takes leave of his body—exits through the sacred opening in the center of the brain known as the *sahasrar.*
- Thus he goes forth to join the "Light-Giver"—allows his body to die as if by an act of will. Thus, he brings his embodied existence to a fruitful end—wholly and solely enters the rotund state of the plenteous.

Reverting back to our prior discussions, there are now three principal sources whence the mind is shown to have taken the initiative—given the green light in execution of this incompliant and most arduous task at hand. From:

1. Chopra's Scientific Models: Having been approached by the mind, the soul gets abducted by it, which in turn crosses over to make that all important contact with God.
2. The Rishis Point of View: The Upanishads too purport the same, in that, the Subtle Body (consisting principally of the mind) submits itself to the soul, which in spontaneity thereto unites with the Divine Ground.

3. God: Without any gyration, the Cognitive Lord Sri Krishna too gave the stamp of approval and sanction thereto.

Like a judge or panel of jurors would carefully consider all the pros and cons before handing down a verdict, here too without much deliberations we have reached this general consensus of opinion: That beyond any reasonable doubt, the confederate mind is seen to have come to the aid or rescue of the soul—the balance of probabilities weighing heavily in favor of it being the one consigned the job of handing the soul over to God.

Enabling the soul to accomplish *mission impossible,* all accolades and praises go out to the mind. It is credited with scoring this much "vital assist" in the game-winning goal of life.

GOD OUR SOUL MATE

Inasmuch as the rishis were jubilant when came time to describe this magical and thaumaturgical moment, they were very specific too even in terms of the words chosen to convey their joyous feelings. Eulogistically put, they spoke in the most glorious portrayal thereof—speaking of which here's a beautiful excerpt from the Holy Upanishads:

SIMILES

As the slough of a snake lies cast-off on an anthill,
so too lies the body of a man at the time of death.
Having freed himself from the body,
he becomes one with the Immortal Spirit—
Brahman the Light Eternal!

*   *   *

Whereas bees gather nectars
from many flowering-plants;

> *and whereas these nectars are*
> *combined and made into honey*
> *so much so no one could tell what flowers*
> *they severally came from;*
> *similarly also, man, in the end*
> *forgoes or cedes his individuality*
> *when merged in the Immortal Essence;*
> *wherefore, he cannot differentiate any longer*
> *between himself and God—*
> *nor tell (knoweth) that he is so submerged in Him!*

In bringing down the curtains, I want to pen the mightiest of words in glorification of *nirvana.* And this unavoidably results in some sort of repetition and verbosity cropping up here and there—something I just cannot avoid due to my passion and love for *nirvana.* I want to make it over glaringly clear that it is what life is all about.

BREAKING CONTACT WITH PAIN

> *"When a man has realized the Self*
> *the pure, the immortal, the blissful*
> *what craving can be left in him*
> *that he should take to another body,*
> *full of suffering, to satisfy it?"*
>
> —The Upanishads

Nirvana, in commonality, brings with it complete cessation of all miseries, pains, sorrows, regrets. Then, what's the point in having to take to another birth underlined with grief and displeasure—to achieve what else in this imperfect world.

He who learns of the glory of the Self knows that the ephemeral body is nothing but a stumbling block to enlightenment—an impediment to man's real progress. The mortal frame must not be the main focus or the center of attention—there being this greater good man is so ear-marked and destined for.

Failing to realize the Brahman in you is to live in complete ignorance—subjected still to the vicious and never-ending *Cycle of Birth and Death*. Having freed oneself thereof, all fetters and trammels would be loosened—bonds of grief shattered. And man shall no longer be devoured by death.

Euphemistically put, death presents itself in an innocuous manner to the liberated souls—no different I suppose from the modern day effects of euthanasia. Being relieved of a great burden when this tent is taken down, a Yogi does not feel even the slightest tremor of pain—nor is there any of this gristly fear in all of his heart.

Indifferent to everything, even death he accepts with a tranquil and content heart. As he goes forth to join the Sweet Lord, he does so with the greatest of easy and comfort. Inasmuch as a snake having cast off its slough lies peacefully on an anthill, even so rests the body of a saint at death! Having disengaged himself from his body, he gets inextricably connected to God.

PERMANENT VS. TEMPORARY HAPPINESS

"Here on earth
all wealth one earns is but transitory.
And fleeting too are heavenly enjoyments.
Therefore, he who dies
without having realized the Self
finds no permanent happiness
in any world to which he goes.
Whereas, he who does
finds permanent happiness everywhere."
—The Chhandogya Upanishad

Being the primary goal sought by man, *nirvana* is by far
the most notable and worthwhile endeavor in all of life. It
confers upon man the definitive and pristine gift of immortality: That which is considered the most abiding, enduring and immutable status of all—one that brings the greatest good to man.

Provisional and tentative is everything else in this theater
of change—a world in the material sense that is inherently
transient, defunct, dead. Lacking the essential element of
permanency, the cosmos is simply structured that way, in
that, with the notable exception of the soul, everything else
shall one day be ethereally vaporized—go up in a cloud
of smoke.

Apart from *nirvana,* the next best reward in life comes
heavenly enjoyments—the entering of the *land of the Blest.*
However, this too shall one day come to an end—reason
being it is also of a protempore, fleeting and impermanent
nature.

That being the case then, how can anyone rejoice even
in heavenly enjoyment (or long life for that matter) knowing that what still hangs over his head is the rope of death—
cognizant of the fact that his life shall be ultimately nulli-
fied and intercepted by death one day.

No one would be allowed to ride on the lap of luxury
forever—or life for that matter! Therefore, he who dies
without realizing the Self finds no permanent happiness
in any world to which he goes. It's a clear-cut stipulation
made by the rishis and God—leaving the assertive and discriminating man no other choice but *nirvana.*

There is this insurgence and insurrection to life. We live
in a mundane world thinking it to be the land of milk and
honey when it is not. Therefore, we have to find a way out
of this prison and state of optical illusion—man in his imposing and celebrated walk-of-glory to join the rank-and-

file of the gods.

NIRVANA IN PERSPECTIVE

It's like leading a captive life here on earth—one of incarceration and imprisonment. And seeking to escape it for something better, the sagacious rishis and God opined *nirvana*—the most coveted and imponderable state of all.

Given its overall influence, *nirvana* is even greater than the guerdon feelings one derives being acquitted from the most grievous of crimes—released from prison after serving a life-sentence, or taken off Death's Roll. What a requital, emolument and manumission to speak of!

Ecstatic and rapturous are the sensations procurable by it—an out of this world feeling to tell the Gospel truth. It's the process whereby the soul is expatriated back to its supermundane state of existence—God's Country, Fantasy World, Dreamland. Hence, the purpose or essence of *religion*—a word meaning "to go back."

Committed back to the Holy Trinity or Triad, it is dubbed the deification process. It's where man upon final decoction is idolized as a veritable god—anointed by the Holy Messiah. And in consummation thereof, he forever indemnifies and consolidates his position with the Cynosure Father in heaven.

Instead of being a mere reprieve, the individual is granted complete immunity and impunity thereto. Designated the *Enfranchisement of the Soul,* its an entitlement whereby man becomes the concessionaire of this most wonderful of gifts.

Ineffable peace of mind and repose come to him who fathoms and realizes his own luminary and refulgent Self. But of what greater magnitude is that nostalgic and exotic sentience when one is united with the Father of all Spirits—beatitude itself, life itself, God in person. It's the peace that passeth all understanding.

THE SENSATIONALISM AND PLEASANTRIES

Like an enlightened seer seems a dying or deceased person—ever so much his calm, recollect, serene self. He appears quite content and safe now lying prostrate at the Holy Feet of God. As if inducted into the Hall of Eternity or the recipient of some Holy Investiture, he literally basks in the divine light.

Coming under the auspices or aegis of the Creator, it is an extremely burgeon and buoyant feeling—the individual uninterruptedly bursting at the seams with joy. And frankly speaking, it is such a sensational feeling that one just can't wait to have this experience oneself.

As if in Alchemy, man is transformed into the state of divineness—a condition that augurs well for him in bestowal of the panacea or elixir of life. And in this most beguiled and ravishing state, one is found enveloped by an aura of mystique and luster—whom now fully bolstered by God is exculpated of all inadequacies and transgressions.

Begrudgingly looking down from heaven, it is even the envy of the celestials to see ordinary mortal beings being admitted into the fold of Godhood. And, as if by the second exponent, it also vivifies the very Cupid god of love to witness man being devolved into a god—clothed in the empyrean robe made for him by God.

THE END OF ALL SUPERFICIALITIES

Marking the end of all inadequacies and superficialities, it is the kingly abode surpassing all others. And at that twilight hour, the translucent Self illumines the inner-man and bestows upon him the exalted status of *apotheosis*—the beauteous, golden state that bewitches a charm beyond all telling.

In other words, *nirvana* is the alpha and omega of life—the beatific and quintessential state of being. It stands stately at the vertex or pinnacle of all man's aspirations—the pentagram, zenith or acme point if you will. And having such a pyramidal effect, it is deemed the rank—ultimatum—the end-all and be-all of our human endeavors.

JOY AD INFINITUM

In fulfillment of one's cherished desire for Self or God realization, it enkindles and fills the heart with an un-thinkable sense of gratification—a perennial joy that knows no bounds. And in perpetuity thereof, it is herald a moment of great conviviality, ecstasy and exaltation of the spirit of man—more like having the unremitting floodgates of eternal pleasure flung wide opened.

Having tactically built such a close rapport with God (become one with Him really), the resplendent seeker becomes the votary of sheer bliss and beatification. He is inundated with much pleasureableness and delectation of spirit—reaches the very home of beatitude and contentment.

In short then, *nirvana* is that urbane, paradisiacal, utopian state that effusively ushers in exquisite perceptiveness and effulgence. It's the subliminal state of being where the Christlike one now revels in the Father God—scintillates with emblematic feelings of joy ad infinitum.

CONCLUSION

Beyond all terrestrial happiness then, *nirvana* is by far the most exhilarating experience of all. Like a magic wand, it confers upon man harmonization and divination with the Holy Spirit. And as it rhapsodically and bewitchingly casts its magic spell, one is left consumed by the Holy Ghost.

Irradiating full blessedness, immortality dawns upon us the moment we find our place in the cosmic flow——puts on this diadem or crown of glory. It is the supreme gift nature earnestly waits to lavish upon us. And taking it to be the ex gratia granting by the Providential Hands, *nirvana* leaves our lives fully bedecked and adorned.

And in testimony thereof, found emanating from the bodies of Yogis at the time of death is that redolent and evocative fragrance known as the *odor of sanctity*——the engaging and sweet smell of success. Like a breath of fresh air, man's disenthralled soul lives on in the person of the Paradigm Mother/Father.

Beyond the threshold of all semantics, no amount of words can adequately convey the glory of it all. And words having failed me, I urge you simply to take to the hallowed path recommended herein, which, though less traveled is the only path worth your while——the road that leads back to Godhead.

Allow God to take charge of your life——embrace the unknown with confidence. You are not whom you think you are. You are a child of the most high God.

BUDDHA

Glory be unto him! Buddha was the repertoire of many blessed qualities. And in his charge for *nirvana* or Eternal Life, he was put to the test. Showing the mettle he was made of (muscles of iron and nerves of steels) he irksomely and unabatedly sat down one place for seven consecutive years fully engaged in deep *samadhi* or meditation.

Here's that famous vow of his——a clear demonstration

of his resoluteness:

> *"Let my body dry on this seat,*
> *my skin and bone and flesh be destroyed,*
> *yet shall I not leave my seat*
> *without achieving that rare bodhi (nirvana).*
> *The great mountains may change their positions,*
> *the world may merge in space,*
> *the planets may fall from their orbits,*
> *the oceans may dry up,*
> *but none can move me from my seat under this tree."*

Come whatever may (hell or high waters) he was most determined to find enlightenment in that very birth of his. Having resolved not to get up from his Holy Seat, he, in his relentless pursuit of the final experience, turned his long cherished dream into a reality. Buddha became the magnanimous God he was.

THE ACHARYA

As alluded to earlier, my guru's guru Acharya Srimat Swami Pranavanandaji Maharaj also similarly pledged—took the morose, ascetic *vow of silence*. Ready to move heaven and earth, he, for six consecutive years without sleep, totally confined himself in deep, prolonged *samadhi*.

Stopping at nothing, he stoutheartedly and tenaciously stayed put. He had himself stationed one place, moving not an inch from his holy fundament. Having stemmed the tide, it culminated in the spirit of God descending upon him carte blanche—entered his being in full-fledged power and glory.

Thus the faculties of God became manifested in him. And through the superhuman personality of this Prophet of the New Hindu Age, God carried out his divine mission.

The Acharya became an intermediary—God in operation through his instrumentality.

Professor Ninian Smart brilliantly recaptured the mood when he wrote: "Seated beneath a kadamba tree, he felt himself entered into the Great Illumination culminating in his six years of no-sleep. Incredible as it may sound, he was a master of nirvikalpa samadhi—the deepest imageless trance in which the mystics attains unity with the formless Brahman.

Thus he became an instrument of divine power after merging with the Absolute. On that auspicious full moon night he felt himself overtaken by divine power. It is the belief of Hindus that during full moon the external planetary conditions are more favorable and conducive to the enhancement of inner bliss and power. On that night in the year 1916 his consciousness blossomed beyond imageless contentment into the dynamic ecstasy of Identity-and-Difference. He felt God in action—he felt oneness with God."

Remarkable achievements indeed. Here's two of a multitude of examples of Great Ones who have attained this remarkable feat—they whom by dint of severe austerity experienced the highest state of subliminal bliss. These were God-men. And they have proven the premise correct—man can indeed be devolved into gods.

Our penance though ought not to be of the same magnitude or severity as theirs. They came as emissaries of God with the mission to lead the denizens of the world unto the path of salvation. Our aspiration is simply to become men of God—not God-men as they were.

JOURNEY'S END

The Vedas begin and end with the one proclamation: *Oh man, know thyself.* And according to the rishis it is the *summum bonum* of our human existence. And this is supported also by the behest of the oracle at Delphi in the statement: *Gnothe scanton*—"know thyself." And the Sufi aspirant too declares: *An-al-Haq*—"I am god."

And one of the greatest sayings of Jesus too bears the truth of it all when he issued the final proclamation of his:

"I and my father are one!"

And here's yet another conclusive Biblical attestation in support of the theory of *Life after Death*. It's a passage taken from one of St. Paul's letters found in the *New Testament:*

"I tell you this my friends:
Flesh and blood cannot inherit the Kingdom of God.
Nor can decay inherit immortality.
Look, I am declaring a mystery to you:
We shall not all die,
but we shall all of us be changed,
in a moment, in a twinkling of an eye,
at the final trumpet sound.
For the trumpet shall sound
and the dead shall be raised up immortal,
and we shall be changed.
For this perishable body must be clothed
with that which does not perish,
and this mortal body must put on immortality.
Then shall come to pass the saying that is written:
Death is swallowed up in victory.
Where, oh death, is thy victory?
Death, where is thy sting?"

We read in the *Bible* too that Jesus died for our sins, buried and was raised on the third day from the dead. This is not to say that one is raised literally or in the physical sense of the word. The body does in fact perish upon burial or cremation. But, in a figurative or spiritual sense, one can certainly be raised from the dead. Putting on the Subtle or Astral Body, he proceeds to the hereafter in this transcendental state of being.

The Hindu philosophy made it abundantly clear that man can conquer death and gain everlasting life. It may be true also that the *Bible* and Christianity does not systematically build around the theme. However, its teachings nonetheless do hint or entertain the possibility.

FINAL THOUGHTS

Getting ready now to take leave of my august readers, I wholeheartedly trust that you've   found your experience reading this book both informative and pleasurable. And as purported by the theory of Universalism I pray that:

> *May we all be ultimately saved*
> *by the sweet grace of God.*
> *May each and everyone of us attain*
> *the final beatitude of nirvana.*
> *May God's benign blessings be with us,*
> *forever and ever more!*

I conclude with these final thoughts: First, this beautiful poem, then an equally beautiful extract from the *Holy Bible*—ending finally with a poem from noble laureate Rabindranath Tagore.

> *Birth and death are two illusory scenes*
> *in the drama on the stage of life.*
> *No one is really ever born—*
> *nor does anyone ever die.*
> *Death is like deep-sleep—*
> *birth like being awakened again.*

And so man goes round-and-round.
over-and-over again
the Wheel of Birth and Death.
Do not be afraid of death,
for if you must know, life is continuous.
To the one who is born, death is certain—
inasmuch as birth is for the dead.
A flower may fade,
but its sweet fragrance remains afloat.
And so too the body may perish,
but the immortal Aroma lives on!
Learn to distinguish the real from the unreal.
Give up the ephemeral body and hold on unto the soul—
the one deathless and birthless.
Free yourself from this prison of optical delusion
this Wheel or Cycle of Birth and Death
by merging in the Immortal Essence—God.

Appointed by God as his trusted messenger, St. Paul in Book 2 Corinthians 5: 1-10, wrote this letter to Christians in Corinth and all of Greece—which this instant should arouse in you an irresistible urge to take to the prescribed path enunciated by the Sweet Lord:

"For we know that when this tent
we live in now is taken down—
when we die and leave these bodies—
we will have wonderful bodies in heaven,
homes that will be ours forever more,
made for us by God himself,
and not by human hands.
How weary we grow of our present bodies.
That is why we look forward eagerly to the day
when we shall have heavenly bodies
which we shall put on like new clothes.

For we shall not be merely spirits without bodies.
These earthly bodies make us groan and sigh,
but we wouldn't like to think of dying
and having no bodies at all.
We want to slip into our new bodies
so that these dying bodies will, as it were,
be swallowed up by everlasting life.
This is what God has prepared for us and,
as a guarantee, he has given us his Holy Spirit.
Now we look forward with confidence
to our heavenly bodies,
realizing that every moment we spend
in these earthly bodies is time spent away
from our eternal home in heaven with Jesus.
We know that these things are true
by believing, not by seeing.
And we are not afraid,
but are quite content to die,
for then we will be home with the Lord.
So our aim is to please him always in everything we do,
whether we are here in this body
or away from this body
and with him in heaven.
For we must all stand before Christ to be judged
and have our lives laid bare before him.
Each of us will receive whatever he deserves
for the good or bad things he has done
in his earthly body."

Verses taken out of the pages of Tagore's *Gitanjali:*

"Of that moment I was not made aware—
the moment I first crossed the threshold of this life.
Nor was I made aware of the power that made me
opened-out into the vast mystery of life—

> *bloomed like a bud in the forest at midnight.*
> *But in the morning when I looked upon the light,*
> *I momentarily felt like no stranger in this world—*
> *for the Inscrutable had taken me into its arms*
> *in the person of my own sweet, loving mother.*
> *And even so in death too,*
> *the same unknown will reappear as ever known to me.*
> *And because I love this life,*
> *death too I shall love!*
> *A babe cries when the mother takes her breast away—*
> *only to find consolation in the other the next moment!"*

We are no orphans in this world. If the earthborn, biological mothers know how to give consolation to their children, how much more wouldn't the Inscrutable protect us disappearing into the fathomless abyss of nothingness—how much more wouldn't He reappear to usher us into the richly deserved Kingdom of His!

Therefore, without dilly-dallying any more, may we act today—have our toes and heels dug firmly in. It does you no good when God-realization is in the blood, but the veins run dry. As long as there is life, keep the dream alive—man who comes specially equipped by God with the wherewithal's to do better. God Bless.

Glossary

Arjuna: The one to whom Lord Sri Krishna related the *Gita*.

Artha: The acquisition of wealth.

Atman: The Sanskrit word for *soul*.

Brahmacharya: The first period of life or *student life*.

Brahman: The manifested power of God.

Dharma: The right course of action.

Gita: The Hindu Bible.

Grihastha: The second stage of life or *house-holder life*.

Gross Body: The physical body.

Kaama: Pleasure.

Leela: The play or drama of God.

Maharshi Mahesh Yogi: The one who promoted *transcendental meditation* in the West.

Maya: Illusion.

Moksha: Salvation—the state of oneness with God.

Nachiketa: The young lad with whom the *god of death* had spoken.

Nirvana: The state of oneness with the formless Brahman (God).

Om: The primeval sound or *word* that existed at the beginning of times.

Prakriti: The principle of consciousness in beings.

Prana: A highly complex, subtle form of energy or *life-breath*.

Preya: The path that leads to *pleasure*.

Rishi: The spiritual masters of India.

Sagittal Suture: A tiny fissure or opening at the crown of the head through which the soul of the enlightened one exits at the time of death.

Sannyas: The final stage of life—a period of renunciation.

Shreya: The path of life that is beneficial to man.

Subtle Body: It is comprised of the *mind, intellect* and *ego*.

Surya Namaskar: Sun-worship.

Turiya: The Fourth State of consciousness, apart from *waking, dreaming* and *dreamless sleep*.

Yama: The Hindu *god of death*.

Bibliography

Chopra, Deepak, *How to Know God*. New York, Random House, 2000.

—, *Ageless Body Timeless Mind*. New York, Harmony Books, 1993.

Eknath, Easwaran, *Dialogue with Death: A Journey Through Consciousness*. Mumbai, Jaico Publishing House, 2002.

Gambhirananda, Swami, *Eight Upanishad with the Commentary of Sankaracharya*, 2 vols., Calcutta, 1958.

Ninian, Smart, and Purnananda, Swami, *Prophet of a New Hindu Age*. London, George Allen and Unwin, 1985.

Prabhavananda, Swami, and Isherwood, Christopher, *Bhagavad Gita: The Song of God*. Chennai, Sri Ramakrishna Math, 1969.

Yogananda, Paramahansa, *Autobiography of a Yogi*. Los Angeles, Self-Realization Fellowship, 1998.

Yogi, Maharshi Mahesh, *Science of Being and Art of Living*. New York, Signet Books, 1968.

Index